Pocket Guide to
Contact Lenses

Pocket Guide to
Contact
Lenses

Nigel Burnett Hodd
BSc. (Hons), F.B.C.O., D.C.L.P.

Arlington Books
King St, St James's
London

POCKET GUIDE TO CONTACT LENSES
First published 1988 by
Arlington Books (Publishers) Ltd
King St, St James's
London SW1

© *Nigel Burnett Hodd 1988*

British Library Cataloguing-in-Publication Data
Hodd, Nigel Burnett
  Pocket guide to contact lenses
  1. Contact lenses
  I. Title
  617.7'523

  ISBN 0–85140–734–X

Printed and bound in Great Britain by
Richard Clay, Suffolk

This special edition has been sponsored by CooperVision Optics Limited in aid of the appeal for the Institute of Optometry

Contents

Introduction

Successful wearers of contact lenses find it easy to explain why contact lenses are better than spectacles. They find that wearing contact lenses makes them less introverted and more outward going and fun to be with. I shall never forget a twenty six year old city gentleman who, when fitted with contact lenses, was so overjoyed with his new personality that he returned especially to shake my hand and express his total joy. His whole life had changed; girls were suddenly finding him attractive and were falling over themselves to go out with him.

Contact lenses look good and feel good. Although modern spectacles can be a lot of fun it is great to lose dependence on them and come out from behind the shades.

When you first get lenses keep telling yourself 'I want to look good and feel good'. The early trials and tribulations will fade into insignificance as you enjoy the freedom that lenses give. This book will help you overcome problems and to understand what you are doing.

Who invented contact lenses (or 'invisible glasses' as the Chinese call them)?
The original idea has been credited to Leonardo da Vinci.

He is supposed to have stuck his head in a bath full of water and discovered that he could see better. The water acted as a crude lens. He then spent a lot of time trying to devise a way to stick small transparent buckets of water onto his eyes!

It was left to an Englishman, Sir John Herschel, Astronomer Royal, in 1845, to work out the basic optical principles of contact lens design, but he never actually made a lens.

Forty-two years later a German artificial eye maker named F. E. Muller made the first contact lens, not to assist vision but to protect an eye that had had its eyelids removed during cancer surgery. This early lens prevented the loss of the eye and was used for twenty years.

A year later, in 1888, a Swiss named Dr. Fick and another German, August Muller, simultaneously made the first lenses to correct a visual defect. Their early efforts, made from blown glass, produced lenses that were so uncomfortable that they could be tolerated for only thirty minutes even when cocaine was used to deaden the pain!

By 1932, the German firm Zeiss was making fitting sets of lenses, and a Hungarian named Josef Dallos made the first glass lenses from moulds he took of living eyes. Dallos moved to London before the war and was instrumental in many advances. Even today there are people still wearing his glass lenses.

In 1942 C.W. Dixey & Son Ltd, a British firm of Dispensing Opticians and instrument makers, invented the ground plastic haptic lenses which were the forerunners of today's hard lenses.

Whereas glass lenses covered the white of the eye, the use of perspex led to the development of smaller lenses that only covered the cornea (the transparent window in front of the iris).

It was soon realised that the smaller the lens was made, the greater the wearing time.

In the 1950s Contact Lens Practitioners devised sophisticated lens designs to enable bifocal spectacle wearers and people with astigmatism to wear contact lenses successfully.

It has been shown that 70% of people who wish to wear hard lenses are completely successful. Those who fail either cannot get used to the initial gritty feeling or develop some form of rejection in the first few months of use. A few are too troubled by dust or bright sunlight. Until 1965 these unlucky people returned reluctantly to wearing spectacles.

What has happened since then to make contact lens wear a successful proposition for the vast majority of people? The answer lies in material technology. Wichterle and Lim, two Czechoslovak researchers, developed the soft contact lens. The idea was purchased and developed by the National Patent Corporation of America. Since then hard plastic technology has also taken off with the development of gas-permeable plastics that allow air to seep through to the eye.

What is lacking to the new contact lens wearer is not a good choice of contact lens materials but this book – *Pocket*

Guide to Contact Lenses. It will give you the information you need to enable you to decide whether contact lenses are for you or, if you are already a contact lens wearer, it will help you to understand them better. If you have tried lenses and are back in glasses it will give you the incentive to try again. Keep this book with you and be sure not to lend it to anyone – like the A–Z maps it will 'walk' given the chance!

The author wishes to acknowledge the help given to him in the preparation of this book by the following people: His wife, Rita; his father, Freddie; Dr Joshua Josephson; Mr R. Loveridge.

Chapter 1
Understanding Your Eyes

A contact lens is a small, shell-like disc that fits between the eyelids and the eye. It is shaped to fit to the front of the eye so that it not only feels comfortable but corrects the vision. It moves with the eye to give the same visual freedom enjoyed by people with normal eyesight.

Let us consider how your eye works. Take a look at the two diagrams of the eye, 1.1 and 1.2. The eye is an independent ball that is held into the eye socket by six muscles, the optic nerve and various tendons and connective tissue.

The inside of the eye contains various jellies and water (Diagrams 1.1 and 1.2). At the front of the eye is the main lens called the cornea. Behind it is a variable opening or aperture called the pupil. The coloured part of the eye, the iris, opens and shuts to let in more or less light. There are special muscles behind the iris that adjust the crystalline lens to alter the focus of the eye for distance or reading. Well behind that is the retina onto which the image is focused. Millions of little light sensitive cells, called rods, pick up the light and thousands more, called cones, detect colour. Millions of little nerves transmit the information down the optic nerve to the brain. Because there are two eyes, the brain is not only able to perceive light and different colours but also sees in 3-D so that we can judge distances and speeds.

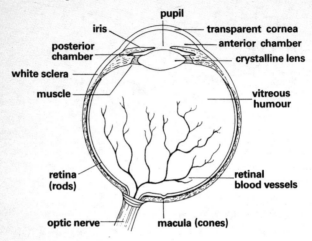

1-1 Cross Section of Eye

The eyes not only rotate to see left, right, up and down in total unison but also have the ability to turn in towards each other to see close objects (convergence). The eyes are rotated by six muscles which are controlled by three nerves. One of these nerves also controls the blinking mechanism of the eyelids. We blink on average fifteen times a minute to keep the front of the eye clean and moist. A further nerve controls the amount of tears produced from the tear gland. The tears wash over the front of the eye.

There are various things that can go wrong with your eyes. There can be faults in the brain or in the nerves leading to and from the brain. There can also be problems in the tissue surrounding the eyes and in the tear system.

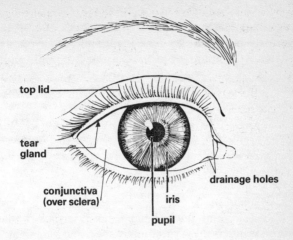

1–2 Front View of eye

The eyes are not always a perfect shape or size and as a result sight defects occur. These are:

1. Short Sight (Myopia)
This is the most common eye defect. It occurs if the eyeball grows too big or if the cornea is too curved. Essentially, the images going into the eye are focused in front of the retina. A diminishing (negative) lens has to be put in front of the eye to push the focus further back onto the retina. People who wear spectacles to correct short sight appear to have smaller eyes behind their glasses than they really have.

2. Long Sight (Hypermetropia)
This is especially common in young people because it is due to the eye being too small, i.e. too short, or due to the

cornea not being curved enough. As the eye grows the condition may lessen. Uncorrected long sight often leads to overfocusing of the eyes. This in turn may cause one eye to turn inwards (squint) or to one eye not developing properly (lazy eye). The images going into the eye are focused behind the retina. The eye tries to refocus the images and considerable eyestrain results. A magnifying (positive) lens has to be put in front of the eye to focus the images further forward onto the retina. People who wear spectacles to correct long sight appear to have larger eyes behind their glasses than they really have.

3. *Astigmatism*

People often think that astigmatism is a serious eye condition. In fact, it is just a variation of short and long sight. The shape of the front of the eye is oval like a rugby ball instead of being round. Some eyes are born out of shape, some grow like it during the teenage years. Some eyes even grow out of it during the teenage years! In astigmatism the image on the retina is totally out of focus and distorted. To correct it a distorted lens has to be put in front of the eye to cancel out the eye's distortion and bring the image into focus. It is not so easy to spot people who wear spectacles to correct astigmatism but if they will let you look through their glasses hold them at arms length and rotate them. Straight lines will appear to wobble as you rotate the lenses.

4. *Old Sight (Presbyopia)*

As people age the crystalline lens begins to solidify. This happens earlier if the eye is exposed to excess sunlight for long periods! For those living in Britain all their lives, at around the age of forty five the fibrous jelly becomes too thick and solid to change focus from distance to reading. The muscles pulling the lens do not wear out – they try even harder. By the time we are sixty five the lens becomes totally hard and in some people it begins to go opaque (a condition called cataract). So, at forty five, reading spectacles are needed that gradually need strengthening until the maximum is reached. When a cataract is removed a plastic lens may be implanted surgically into the eye, a contact lens may be used, or spectacles will be needed.

Bifocals are worn to correct for distance and reading simultaneously. Old sight should not be confused with long sight. People with presbyopia can be spotted by the fact that they wear bifocals and so look down to read or they have a pair of spectacles in their purse or top pocket to put on for reading. They also complain that newspapers are not printed properly, that the light is not good enough and that their arms seem too short!

HOW DOES A CONTACT LENS WORK?

A contact lens works by simply altering the effective shape of the cornea. It sits on the front of the eye. The gap between the lens and the eye fills with tears to create a liquid lens and this plastic/liquid lens combination corrects the sight defect.

Diagram 1.3 shows the principle of a contact lens on the eye. The lens is specially shaped to match the average shape of the cornea. The liquid between the lens and the eye not only acts as a lens but it also creates surface tension. Just like a piece of wet polythene on a kitchen surface it sticks and will not come off easily! The eyelids blink up and down and the lens floats up and down on the cornea as tears are

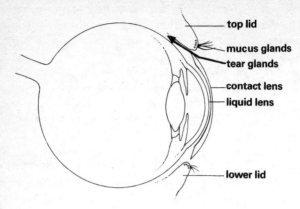

top lid
mucus glands
tear glands
contact lens
liquid lens
lower lid

1–3

washed over the front of the lens and flushed behind the lens. The lids secrete grease and mucus from special glands and tears come from the large tear gland above the eye (the lacrimal gland). It is this gland that goes berserk when you cry!

The secret of a safe and well-fitting contact lens is that it should settle onto the front of the eye to give good vision, it should move a little when you blink so that tears wash around it, it should not dig into the eye or lids and once it has adapted to the lens the eye should not feel it.

Chapter 2
Types of Contact Lens.

Although the general public categorise contact lenses into hard and soft lenses there are, in fact, five principle types:
1. Corneal Hard Lenses.
2. Gas-Permeable Lenses.
3. Scleral or Haptic Lenses.
4. Low Water Content Soft Lenses.
5. High Water Content Soft Lenses.
Types 1 – 3 are rigid lenses. Types 4 – 5 are soft and flexible.

1. Corneal Hard Lenses

These are made of Perspex (acrylic resin) and are colloquially called 'Hard Lenses'. Corneal hard lenses are usually about 9 millimetres in diameter though they can vary in size from 6 to 12 millimetres. When they are less than 8 mm they may be called 'micro-corneals'. Perspex is a very versatile and durable material. It is easy and cheap to manufacture by conventional methods. It can be made in a large range of colours, needs very little looking after and can be repolished when scratched. With reasonable care perspex lenses will last on average 7 years, though it is not uncommon to find people using 20 year old lenses.

Corneal hard lenses have two basic flaws as far as the eye is concerned. Perspex is impervious to water and gases and is a poor conductor of heat. As a result, the eyes have to adapt to a reduced oxygen supply by building up the wearing time over several weeks. People may experience difficulty wearing their spectacles after removing this type of lens because the cornea may be slightly swollen. Considerable spectacle blur can occur in the early stages of adaptation but once fully adapted you should be able to see properly with your original spectacles. If you have worn this type of lens for many years and you cannot see through your spectacles this may be a sign that your corneas are suffering from lack of oxygen. You should return to your practitioner for reassurance on this point. It may be that you should be refitted with gas-permeable lenses.

Advantages of Corneal hard Lenses are:
(a) They are usually the cheapest lenses initially and long term.
(b) They are easy to look after.
(c) They are very durable and can be repolished.
(d) Once fitted successfully, the lens prescription rarely has to be changed.
(e) Generally they give better vision than soft lenses.

Problems with Corneal Hard Lenses are:
(a) They take a bit of getting used to.
(b) Dust can get under the lens.
(c) They are easily lost.
(d) You may be unable to wear spectacles as an alternative.
(e) The eyes become sensitive to light and hot atmospheres.

(f) The lenses have to be worn for a set period of time every day.

2. *Gas-Permeable Lenses*

Gas-permeable Lenses were developed to allow more oxygen to reach the cornea. They are also better conductors of heat. Adaptation to these lenses is much quicker than with corneal hard lenses because the eyes can breathe better. Because gas-permeable lenses absorb a small amount of water they must be stored in the correct solution when not being worn.

The first gas-permeable lenses were made of cellulose acetate butyrate (C.A.B.) which is the same plastic as is used for toothbrush handles. The lenses can be pure C.A.B. or mixed with Perspex for durability. C.A.B. has not proved to be very durable as it scratches easily but with repolishes the lenses should last an average of four years.

The next gas permeable lenses to be developed were a mixture of silicone and perspex. Silicone acrylates are more gas permeable than C.A.B. but it has been found that silicone attracts protein deposits from the tears necessitating more rigorous cleaning.

The most recent silicone acrylate materials have fluorocarbons added to make them more resistant to the formation of deposits whilst keeping the oxygen permeability high. Some of these materials are so gas permeable that it is possible to wear the lenses even when asleep. This can be very useful if you want to take a nap on the bus or train. You should never wear your lenses overnight unless you have been specifically advised by your practitioner that it is safe for you to do so.

The advantages of Gas-Permeable lenses are:
(a) Adaptation is quick and wearing time can be varied.
(b) Usually unaffected by bright sunlight and smoky atmospheres.
(c) Most suitable type of contact lens for dryish eyes.
(d) Generally give better vision than soft lenses.

Problems with gas-permeable lenses are:
(a) Because they are rigid you still have to get used to wearing them but they are easier than hard lenses.
(b) Dust can get under the lens.
(c) Easily lost and broken.
(d) Deposits may form on the surface of the lens.
(e) The lenses must be carefully cleaned and stored in solution.
(f) Sometimes give less good vision than corneal hard lenses.

3.　Scleral or Haptic Lenses

Scleral lenses were the original style of lens first made one hundred years ago in glass. Today the lenses are made in Perspex. The lenses are about 23mm across and fit onto the white of the eye (the sclera) so that the optical part in the centre straddles the cornea but does not touch it. The lens usually has a hole or vent in it to let air behind the lens so that the cornea can breathe. These lenses are used where there is a risk of the lenses falling out, e.g. in water sports, or sometimes where no other lens has worked. They are not always intended to be worn all day. Such lenses are also used to make a false eye. A new eye can be painted onto the scleral lens in any position and will look remarkably like the other real eye!

Scleral lenses are fitted either using special fitting sets of trial lenses or by taking an impression of the eye. Drops are used to anaesthetize the eye so that impression material can be pressed against it. It sounds unpleasant but, in fact, it is quite fun.

The lenses usually last a lifetime.

Advantages of Scleral Lenses
(a) Very safe for sport.
(b) Arthritic or partially sighted people find these lenses the easiest to handle.
(c) When a lens is required to cover a disfigured eye, scleral lenses usually give the best appearance.
(d) Unlikely to fall out.
(e) Scleral lenses are easy to look after and are very durable.

Problems with Scleral Lenses
(a) Wearing time may be restricted to five hours.
(b) Some people find it awkward to put these lenses in at first.

Introduction to Soft Lenses

As the name implies, these lenses are made of soft plastics which mould to the eye. Soft lenses contain water and, if allowed to dry out, shrink to a smaller size and become brittle. The water content of soft lenses varies between 28% and 85% depending on the material composition. Soft lenses are very comfortable from the first day they are worn and are not troubled by dust. As a result, they are often the ones people think they would like. Soft lenses are usually between 12mm and 15mm in diameter and completely clear. Some soft lenses can be tinted to enhance eye colour (see chapter 10).

4.   *Low Water Content Soft Lenses*

Low water content soft lenses are usually made out of a material called H.E.M.A. (2-Hydroxyl-Ethyl-Methacrylate) which contains about 38% water. The lenses can be made standard thickness (over 0.10mm), ultra-thin (less than 0.10mm) or hyper-thin (0.05mm or less).

Low water content soft lenses are usually the soft lens of first choice because any increase in water content reduces the life expectancy of the lens. They are often the cheapest soft lens to buy in the first place and the cheapest to maintain (see chapter 4). However, the practitioner will prescribe the lens he feels is most suited to your eyes.

Advantages of Low Water Content Soft Lenses.
(a) Very comfortable to wear.
(b) Do not break as easily as high water content soft lenses.
(c) Last longer than high water content soft lenses.
(d) Standard thickness lenses are easy to handle.
(e) Cheapest type of soft lens initially and long term.

Problems with Low Water Content Soft Lenses.
(a) Lifespan of these lenses is, at the most, two years.
(b) Particularly prone to protein deposits.
(c) May contribute to small increases in prescription (myopic creep).
(d) Hyper-thin lenses are particularly difficult to handle.

5. *High Water Content Soft Lenses.*

Imagine a soft lens is like a sponge. A sponge is full of holes. A low water content lens has an enormous number of extremely small holes and a high water content lens has bigger holes. The higher the water content the bigger the holes have to be in order to retain more water. High water content lenses contain from 50% to 85% water. The higher the water content the more suitable the lens is for overnight wear. Your practitioner will discuss with you the merits and risks of extended wear and will either recommend nightly removal or longer periods of wear ranging from occasional overnight wear to as long as three months. Never wear any lens overnight unless you have been specifically advised that it is safe to do so!

Generally speaking, unless there is a good reason for longer periods of wear, most practitioners will recommend weekly removal of extended wear lenses.

The expression 'daily +' is used to describe occasional overnight or prolonged wear. This means that if you are caught out and cannot remove your lenses you may keep them in for the occasional night. It is not intended that you be caught out every night!

General Points on Extended Wear

It is not for this handbook to put forward arguments for or against extended wear. There are powerful opinions within the medical and optometric professions so you must be guided by your practitioner. However there is no doubt that there is a greater risk of problems with the eyes from extended wear mainly because people keep the lenses in too long and do not replace the lenses frequently enough.

You must be hygienic when putting the lenses in, follow the instructions on cleaning the lenses whilst in the eye and take them out to rest the eyes when instructed. Not all eyes will accept extended wear so you should look at your eyes every morning and apply the motto 'if in doubt, take them out'. More frequent lens replacements are needed with extended wear so some practitioners will advise planned replacement.

Planned Replacement

Once you have worn extended wear lenses for two months or so your practitioner will be able to assess how often your lenses will need to be replaced. On the whole, the general consensus of opinion with extended wear is that lenses should be replaced at three monthly intervals so your practitioner will plan to see you at either three monthly intervals when he will issue you with new lenses or at six monthly intervals when he will issue you with two sets. This is called 'planned replacement'.

Disposable Lenses

In the most recent planned replacement system, introduced in 1988, lenses are removed weekly and thrown away. There is then no need to use cleaners or solutions other than a sterile saline wash. Packs of lenses are issued at the three monthly visit.

Advantages of High Water Content Lenses

(a) The wearing time can be tailored to suit your lifestyle.
(b) May be used for daily + or extended wear with your practitioner's consent.
(c) Easy to wear in hot, dry atmospheres.

(d) Easiest soft lens to wear on a daily basis if the eyes are naturally slightly dry.

Disadvantages of High Water Content Lenses
(a) The higher the water content the less durable the lenses become.
(b) The higher the water content the more prone to contamination the lenses become.
(c) Caring for the lenses can be fiddly.
(d) The most expensive type of lenses to upkeep.
(e) You must be prepared to visit your practitioner more frequently with this type of lens.

General Points – Soft versus Rigid Lenses

Advantages of Soft Lenses.
(a) Dust does not get under the lenses.
(b) No set wearing time.
(c) Very comfortable initially.
(d) Eye colour can be enhanced.

Advantages of Rigid contact lenses.
(a) Often give better sight.
(b) Lenses last longer on average.
(c) Care systems are cheaper.
(d) Less fiddly to look after.
(e) Less prone to infection.

Chapter 3
Should I Have Contact Lenses?

It is sometimes difficult to decide whether to have contact lenses or not, especially if you have worn spectacles for years. Spectacles may be part of your image. You may have the normal instinct that you do not want to touch your eyes let alone put something in them!

Let us examine the pros and cons of contact lens wear by making a few bold statements about contact lenses and see how spectacles fare.

1. You look better without spectacles on!
In nine out of ten people this is true. Appearance is the major reason people give when wanting contact lenses. However there are people who look very good in spectacles. Spectacles these days can be very fashionable and enjoyable to wear but the same pair won't match every outfit.

2. Contact Lenses are not affected by rain
Spectacles can be a nuisance when they get wet but you can protect them with the right headgear. On windy days spectacles help keep the dust out of your eyes. They are also good protection from dust and splinters when doing D.I.Y.

Contact lenses are kept clean and clear because they are continuously wiped when you blink.

3. Contact Lens Wearers have a free choice of sunglasses
You can wear any sunspecs you like with contact lenses as long as they are good quality and they will also keep dust out of your eyes when it is dry, hot and breezy. Soft Lenses are unaffected by dust and some contact lenses have ultra-violet protection built in.

4. Contact Lenses give better vision than spectacles
This is not necessarily true especially with soft lenses. Fully corrected spectacles will give you a high standard of vision. A contact lens on the eye may get dirty and greasy, obscuring the vision a little and making you blink to clear the vision.Soft lenses flex on the eye and do not always correct the astigmatism, the vision can therefore be worse than spectacles.

If you are short-sighted, contact lenses do not minify the picture in the way that spectacles do so you can see things bigger and therefore better. Conversely, long-sighted people get more magnification with spectacles.

Another factor to consider if you are nearing the age of 43 and on the verge of needing reading spectacles is that contact lens wearers may need reading glasses earlier than spectacle wearers. Because a contact lens sits on the eye, not 2 cm in front of the eye as with glasses, you actually need to focus harder to read.

Short-sighted people can often take their glasses off to read – Something they cannot do when wearing contact lenses.

Nevertheless, most people report being happier with the

vision they get from contact lenses compared to spectacles.

5.   *Contact Lenses give more visual freedom*

Because a contact lens is on the eye it moves with the eye. Wherever the eye looks the lenses look. With spectacles there is a tendency to turn the head so as to keep looking through the centre. Spectacles give distortion and coloured aberrations away from the centre. Spectacle lenses also give reflections that are annoying. Some prescriptions give blind spots particularly if the frame is thick. Others restrict the field of view. Frames with thick sides blinker the vision. Some bifocal spectacles give a jack-in-the-box effect when you look down.

People report far greater visual freedom with contact lenses compared to spectacles.

6.   *Spectacles often hurt the nose and ears and they slip down all the time*

It is true that spectacles can be a confounded nuisance especially if you have sensitive or oily skin. Also not everybody can get a really comfortable spectacle fitting. The bridge of your nose is not always a good place to put spectacles yet it is all we have! The ears were designed to listen with not to hang spectacles from. However, some people prefer the discomfort of spectacles to all the bother of looking after contact lenses. Spectacles are easy to look after and if you do not have to wear them all the time they are no real trouble.

7.   *Contact lenses do not steam up during sport or in a moist atmosphere*

Spectacles can get steamed up when you get hot or are in the bathroom, but you get used to it. Although contact lenses should not steam up they can get greasy sometimes and this may be just as irritating as spectacles that steam up. It is easier to take glasses off to clean them than to remove and clean contact lenses.

8.   *Contact Lenses are better for sports*

This is generally true though some sportsmen or women do better in spectacles, e.g. Dennis Taylor in snooker, Martina Navratilova in tennis. Swimmers should not wear contact lenses (except sclerals) unless they wear goggles.

All squash players, whether they wear contact lenses or not, should wear proper eye protection to avoid damage from the ball or your opponent's racket.

Provided you wear protective goggles, contact lenses give great freedom to skiers. Spectacles can be a nuisance behind goggles. It is not true that contact lenses freeze onto your eyes when skiing.

Here is a list of sports together with the appropriate contact lens for that type of sport:

Abseiling	Sclerals
Badminton	All types.
Cricket and Baseball	All types with U-V inhibitor.
Darts	All types, beware of atmosphere.
Fencing	All types.
Fishing	All types with polaroid sunglasses. U–V inhibitor good.
Hang-gliding and Parachuting	Soft best to avoid dust, or use goggles.
Hockey	All types.
Horseriding	All types, soft best.

Jogging and Athletics	All types.
Rugby and American Football	Soft or Sclerals.
Scuba Diving	All types with goggles.
Shooting	Rigid best.
Skiing	All types with U-V inhibitor and goggles.
Snooker and Pool	Rarely works for professionals.
Soccer	Soft best.
Squash	All types with eye protection.
Table Tennis	All Types.
Tennis	All types, U-V inhibitor good.
Volleyball	Soft best.
Water sports	Sclerals.
Wrestling and Judo	Soft.

TAKING THE PLUNGE

Everybody is different and it is not possible to be sure how you will get on until you try. Most people who try, succeed and they also report that 'it was not as bad as I expected, I wish I had done it years ago!'.

If you are not sure whether to try, talk to your usual eye care practitioner. Does he think your prescription is suitable? If he does not have any contact lens knowledge ask him to find out. Then talk to people who have lenses. How have they got on? What type do they have? Did they try ones that did not work? Gradually other peoples' experiences will give you some confidence but do not believe that everything they tell you will apply to you. You are different!

You may now have an idea of what type of lens you think

you want. Now comes the difficult bit. Who should you consult to get lenses? You cannot beat personal recommendation from friends, your optometrist, dispensing optician, ophthalmic medical practitioner, ophthalmologist or general practitioner.

Did the name of one contact lens practitioner keep cropping up? Was he highly recommended or to be avoided? Your doctor in particular will tend to see the problems created by contact lenses such as infections!

Once you have decided who to see then make an appointment for contact lens assessment and fitting and ask for any information that is available (Leaflets, Costs, etc.). You will be interested in cost but do not make it the only factor. Cheap is not necessarily the best. You need to know what services are included in the charges and what services are extra.

If all else fails and you are not sure who to see then there are optometrists and dispensing opticians who have specialist fitting qualifications after their names. In the U.K., optometrists have D.C.L.P. (The Diploma of Contact Lens Practice) and dispensing opticians have (Hons)C.L. or C.L. (A.B.D.O.) after their other letters.

There is a basic difference in the responsibilities of an optometrist fitting contact lenses and a dispensing optician. The optometrist will examine your eyes, decide if lenses are suitable, prescribe them, and then fit them himself. The dispensing optician will work to the spectacle prescription given to him by an optometrist, ophthalmic medical practitioner or ophthalmologist and when he is satisfied that lenses are successfully fitted he will refer you back to the prescriber. One has to decide therefore whether to let one person take total control of your eyes or to let two people share the responsibility.

There are also a few ophthalmologists (doctors who specialise in eye diseases) who fit their own contact lenses. This can occur in private practice but is more likely to happen with medical cases in eye hospitals.

As I am an optometrist and I carry out the whole function, in the next two chapters I shall go through the whole process from the intitial eye examination, through all the special tests relating to contact lens suitability, the fitting and the follow-up care as I would do it.

Chapter 4
Getting Your Lenses

Step 1. Making the Appointment
It is very unusual not to have to make an appointment for
contact lenses. You may even need to make two appointments if the prescriber is not the fitter. In the normal way an
hour needs to be allowed for the examination and the fitting. You may also be asked to try some lenses for anything
up to five hours so make sure you have left the day fairly
free. It is even possible that extra time may be taken on the
first day to teach you how to insert and remove lenses. The
receptionist will be trained to explain to you the appointments needed for initial assessment.

Step 2. Getting to Know the Prescriber
Once you have settled in the consulting room tell your
optometrist or ophthalmologist all about your eyes and why
you are consulting him or her. Tell him a brief family history
of eye problems and about your general health. If you take
drugs, tell him what they are and why you take them. He
will want to know about your working environment, your
sporting activities, how much television you watch,
whether you drive and all about your hobbies. He might
want to measure you old spectacles and contact lenses if
you have them.

He will also discuss factors relating to contact lenses. He will want to know why you want them and whether you want to wear them all the time or just for social uses. Even if he does not do the fitting he should still know about the types of lens that will suit your needs.

Step 3.   *The First Test*

The optometrist will ask you to read the letter chart with each eye in turn and then he will put a special frame on your face to hold lenses or put a big machine full of lenses in front of your eyes. Either way he will look into your eyes with a special torch called a retinoscope. This instrument shines a light through the pupil which is reflected off the back of the eye and he sees a red image. By putting lenses in front of the eyes he alters the appearance of the red image until he knows your prescription. He then moves on to the subjective test (step 4).

Step 4.   *Getting Comfortable Sight*

This is the bit where you do the work. The retinoscope prescription is fine-tuned by asking you a succession of questions usually comparing two different lenses. He will keep saying 'Which is better one or two?'. Eventually, with your help, the optometrist will find the best lens for each eye and then he will check them together making fine adjustments to maximise comfort.

He will also check whether your muscles are co-ordinating properly, how strong a lens you need to focus on reading material, VDUs, etc and perhaps whether you have normal colour vision.

Your optometrist will now know what prescription or treatment you need but the examination is not yet over.

Step 5. *Looking Closely at Your Eyes*
The front of your eye is examined under thirty or forty times magnification with an instrument called a slit lamp. Although this is often done as part of a standard eye examination it has particular relevance to the potential contact lens wearer. It is also an instrument used at all aftercare visits to ensure that the lenses are not harming the eye in any way. The examination with the slit lamp shows the practitioner many things including:

(a) Whether your tears have the right balance of water and mucus.
(b) Whether there are sufficient tears to maintain contact lenses.
(c) Whether the cornea is clear or whether there are dry patches or scars present.
(d) Whether the cornea is the correct thickness and that all the layers of the cornea are normal.
(e) Whether the blood vessels around the edge of the cornea are normal.
(f) Whether the eyelids are clean and the glands on the edge of the lids are secreting properly.

Step 6. *Taking Your Eye Pressure*
If you have a family history of glaucoma or you are over forty your optometrist will measure your eye pressure. He does this either by pressing a special instrument against the surface of your eye or by puffing air at your eye from a machine. Regular pressure checks will show your optometrist the variation in your eye pressure over the years. He can then detect if it suddenly goes up even if it is still within the safe area before glaucoma occurs.

Step 7.   Checking the Health of Your Eyes
Using an ophthalmoscope, your optometrist will look through your pupil, through the inside of your eye to the retina at the back. This is one of the most important parts of the examination as the eye is the only place in the body where blood vessels and nervous tissue can be clearly seen. Just by looking in with his ophthalmoscope, he can assess the health of your eyes and your body too. In the eye he can see conditions such as cataract and macular degeneration, and by studying the blood vessels and optic-nerve head he may be able to detect conditions such as hypertension, diabetes and glaucoma.

Step 8.   Seeing All Around
Every driver realises the importance of all round vision. Your optometrist will check your ability to see sideways by using either a wand or flashing lights. Any loss of all round vision may be indicative of more serious problems. In particular, he is looking for reduced night vision, visual loss from glaucoma or from a host of general conditions that might not otherwise be detected.

Step 9.   Measuring Your Cornea
Your practitioner will measure the shape of the cornea with a keratometer. This instrument measures the central 3 or 4mms of the cornea to an accuracy of 100th of a millimetre. Sometimes such an instrument will photograph the surface of the cornea with reflections of circles. Whatever is used it tells the practitioner whether the contact lens can be fitted and which sort will give the best vision. At future visits it may also show minute changes in the corneal shape induced by the use of contact lenses.

Step 10. Other Measurements
The practitioner will take other measurements such as the corneal diameter in each eye, the size of the pupil in a darkened and a light room, the distance between the top and bottom lid and how the lids lie in relation to the iris.

Step 11. Putting in the first lens
At this point in the proceedings your practitioner will know what lenses he wants to use. He will know if your eyes are unsuitable for certain lenses and will advise you which sort you should have. He will discuss with you pros and cons of the types available and may even talk about relative costs. It is important here not to get too bogged down in discussions but to get some lenses into your eyes. Once the lenses are in there is plenty of time for talking whilst they settle down.

This part of getting lenses is very individual. It depends on your reaction and it depends on the type of lens you are trying.

Some people can hardly feel the lenses whilst others are more sensitive, but in all cases it should be quite bearable and if you keep calm and confident the initial feeling quickly passes. Your practitioner will know if your reaction is abnormal and will remove the lens very quickly if he is not happy. Even if you react a lot when the lens is first put in it does not mean you will not get used to lenses easily. It just means that you have a well developed nervous system.

If you are trying rigid lenses you will be asked to look down once the lens is in. This reduces the feeling of it catching under the top lid. After five minutes or so you will be able to look straight ahead. Then the other lens is put in!

If you are trying soft lenses they usually feel fairly comfortable immediately. There might be a little stinging at first. Soft lenses, if they are not a suitable fit, may feel worse after half an hour or so.

If you are trying sclerals they feel quite reasonable at first but your eye feels a little uncomfortable after a while. It is an odd sensation but quite acceptable. The practitioner will alter the fitting to ease any discomfort. If he cannot fit you from the fitting set he will take an impression of the eye. As mentioned in chapter 2 taking an impression is quite fun and nothing to worry about.

Depending on your reaction and how well you see, your practitioner will either continue fitting the same type of lens or try other types. Enough time will have been allowed to do this trial fitting as it is the most important part of getting contact lenses.

Step 12.   The tolerance trial
Once your practitioner is happy that he has the best fittings in your eyes and you can see well enough with the trial lenses he may send you out in the fresh air for half an hour or so, or even three to five hours. This is called a tolerance trial. It is not strictly essential but it gives you the time to decide whether you want the lenses and gives your eyes a chance to react to them.

Once the decision to go ahead is made, final lenses can be ordered or issued directly from stock. Soft lenses particularly are often stocked by the practitioner as the number of fitting possibilities is limited and, believe it or not, 80% of people fit into a narrow range of prescriptions.

Step 13.   Learning to live with lenses
The next step is to teach you general lens hygiene, how to

put the lenses in and how to get them out again. You also need to have the care systems explained and instructions given on how to avoid breaking the lenses and how best to look after them. This is such an important subject that I have devoted the whole of chapters 5 and 6 to it.

Maybe, before you get too committed, it is time to explain the costs to you.

The costs involved

There are two costs to consider when buying contact lenses:
(a) The initial fitting and aftercare charges.
(b) The annual cost of maintenance (solutions, insurance, visits and replacement lenses).

(a) What is aftercare?

Contact lenses are not like spectacles. You do not just have them fitted and that is it until you need another pair. A contact lens is a foreign body in your eye that could, if you are unlucky, either be rejected or cause damage to the eye. Your eyesight is too precious to risk damage and your practitioner too conscientious to let you have lenses without follow-up care. The typical visits needed when you first get lenses are listed in table 4.1.

Your practitioner may not exactly agree with these figures. Some practitioners may want more time and some feel less is quite adequate.

Lots of people need attention outside the planned visits. If your practitioner decides to change the type of lens it will involve him in extra material and time costs. Most practitioners even the costs out so that everybody pays the same inclusive charge for a particular type of lens. The inclusive

Table 4.1: Typical Visits Required

	RIGID	SOFT	EXTENDED WEAR
Initial fitting including examination	1 hour	1 hour	1 hour
Tolerance trial and teaching	allow 1 hour	allow 1 hour	allow 1 hour
After 24 hours			15 mins
After 1 week		15–30 mins	15–30 mins
After 2 weeks	15–30 mins		
After a further 3 weeks	15 mins	15 mins	15–30 mins
After a further 6 weeks	15 mins	15 mins	15 mins
After a further 3 months	15–30 mins	15–30 mins	15–30 mins

charge for contact lenses is made up as follows:

material costs

time costs

initial cases and solutions (See chapter 6)

insurance premium or replacement scheme fee (See chapter 12)

Obviously the two major costs are for materials and time. When paying for time you should not imagine that the fees go straight into the practitioner's pocket. Whilst you are in the consulting room or seeing the assistants you are utilising the whole practice. The equipment used is very expensive and the cost of a lens stock may be high too.

(b) Annual Costs

When you add up the cost of solutions, replacement lenses, insurance and necessary check ups it may come to more than you expect. When you get lenses you should be told how long the lenses are likely to last and how often you need to return for check ups.

Table 4.2 attempts to show the annual costs involved. Points are scored under the headings of average lifespan, the loss factor, the breakage factor, the maintenance factor, solution costs and the time factor. Points are scored and the higher the points the lower the annual cost. The lower the points scored the higher the cost. The maintenance factor relates to such things as repolishing rigid lenses and cleaning soft lenses. I have had to use my knowledge and experience to put different emphasis on the points scored. Interestingly, the loss and breakage factors do not add significantly to the annual costs. Generally speaking, the higher the gas permeability or the higher the water content, the higher the cost. The major exception is extended wear where weekly removal reduces the cost of solutions dramatically.

From the table it is easy to see that the most expensive lenses to run are high water content soft daily wear lenses. Extended wear soft lenses cost about the same to run as low water content daily wear soft lenses. All soft lenses cost more than rigid lenses.

Amongst the rigid lenses costs go up as the gas permeability goes up. Sclerals are the cheapest to run, followed closely by hard Perspex lenses.

You can make relative judgements as follows if you wish. In my opinion, if you do everything correctly, using the solutions, attending for check ups and replacing your lenses as

Table 4.2: Annual cost of contact lenses: the greater the points – the lower the cost

MATERIAL	AVERAGE LIFE SPAN (YEARS)	+ POINTS	LOSS FACTOR	+ POINTS	BREAKAGE FACTOR	+ POINTS	MAINTEN- FACTOR	+ POINTS	SOLUTION COSTS RELATIVE + POINTS	TIME FACTOR RELATIVE + POINTS	TOTAL POINTS
HARD PERSPEX	7	36	1 per 2 yrs	2	1 per 5 yrs	5	2 yearly polish	2	8	8	61
CAB & LOW GAS	4	24	1 per 2 yrs	2	1 per 3 yrs	3	1 yearly polish	1	5	6	41
HIGH GAS	2	12	1 per 2 yrs	2	1 per 2 yrs	2	1 yearly polish	1	3	4	24
SCLERALS	12	40	1 per 8 yrs	8	1 per 12 yrs	12	3 yearly polish	3	10	8	81
LOW WATER SOFT	1½	8	1 per 2 yrs	2	1 per year	1	6 mnths clean	½	2	4	17½
HIGH WATER SOFT	¾	4	1 per 2 yrs	2	1 per 9 mths	¾	6 mnths clean	½	1	4	12¼
EXTEND- ED WEAR SOFT	¼	1	1 per year	1	1 per 2 yrs	2	NONE	5	8	1	18

advised, you could reach an average cost in the U.K. by applying the following formula (1988 prices):

Annual cost of maintaining lenses = £2,500 divided by the points scored.

Applying this formula the annual costs for each type of lenses is as follows:

Hard Perspex	£41
Low Gas Permeable	£61
High Gas Permeable	£104
Sclerals	£31
Low Water Content Soft	£143
High Water Content Soft	£204
Soft Extended Wear	£139

Your practitioner can put any figure he feels appropriate instead of £2,500 in the formula. He might feel a higher or a lower figure is appropriate. It will vary from country to country and from area to area of each country. Table 4.1 can only be a rough guideline and remember it does not consider special lenses (chapter 10) or disposables.

Chapter 5
Insertion and Removal

General Hygiene

The most important thing to remember with contact lenses is that they are foreign bodies as far as your eyes are concerned. The lenses must cause some reaction from the eye when they are put in and when they are removed. Lens cleanliness and general hygiene are vital.

Before you handle your lenses or touch your eyes, you should always wash your hands with unperfumed or simple soap and rinse thoroughly. (Also see chapter 9). The hands can be allowed to air dry or dry them on a clean, dust (lint) free towel. To avoid damage to your lenses or eyes nails should be kept clean and short, they certainly should not be sharp or jagged. Hand creams should be avoided and lenses should not be contaminated with perfume or lacquer.

The lenses should be clean in their case having been put away clean after the previous wear.

Once the lenses have been inserted and have settled on the eyes you can apply your make-up, face creams, etc, but still be careful not to contaminate the lenses. Once you are really experienced, you may find it more convenient to put your make-up on first and pop the lenses in afterwards.

Setting up the workstation

It is important to have an area set out with everything to hand for insertion and removal. A dressing table top is not always the best place as it gets very cluttered. A well lit work-surface which has leg space is ideal.

(a) Spread out a soft, white cloth or towel.
(b) Use an adjustable, magnifying make-up mirror.
(c) Have a table lamp that can be directed in the mirror to illuminate your face.
(d) Keep a clean, empty spare case or left and right container permanently on hand.
(e) Keep bottles of all your solutions in the same spot.
(f) Keep a box of unperfumed tissues on hand.
(g) Keep spectacles and their case handy.

Rigid Corneal Lenses

Left handed people should reverse the following instructions.

The steps to follow are:

To put the lenses in, remove the right lens from the right side of the case without scratching it up the side. Prepare the lens for insertion following the instructions given to you by your teacher. This may involve rinsing the lens before applying wetting solution and checking that it is the correct lens.

There is no set rule as to which finger is best used to insert the lens. It depends on your dexterity and the length of your fingers. Most people use the index finger on their favourite hand to insert the lenses into both eyes. Occasionally people will choose to use their right hand for the right eye and the left hand for the left.

5–1 Place Lens on Index finger

Place the lens on the right index finger with the inside of the lens looking at you (Diagram 5.1). Steady the right hand in front of your face coming from below and use the middle finger to pull the lower lid down and to steady the approach of the index finger. At the same time, use the left hand to pull the top lid up and to inhibit the blink. To do this lift the left elbow out and up so that your left hand comes down over the forehead and the fingers can pull up the lid at the lashes (Diagram 5.2).

Now that the top lid is held, the lower lid is being pulled down and the lens is about an inch from your eye, move the lens towards the cornea. While you are doing this look towards the mirror which should be positioned so you are

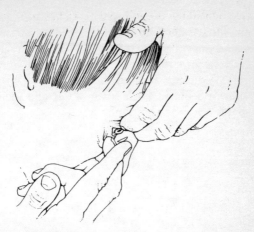

5–2 Putting the Lens in

looking slightly down or look at a point just below the image of the lens in the mirror. This will help you to stop blinking. Put the lens gently on the middle of your eye but DO NOT RELEASE YOUR LIDS, now withdraw the finger, release the top lid and then the bottom lid. Blink and the lens should be in place.

This procedure grows easier with practice but success depends on holding the lids properly and inhibiting the reflex closure of the eye and doing it without hesitation.

Before starting the other eye ensure that the first lens is in place by covering the left eye and seeing if you can see through the lens (Diagram 5.3). If the lens is not in the middle, locate it and recentre it. (See below).

Now follow the same procedure to put in the other lens. It is easiest to use the same hand though you will find your nose tends to get in the way.

Check both lenses are in position (Diagram 5.3), refill the case with fresh solution and replace the tops on the case before leaving the workstation. Remember that case hygiene is as important as lens hygiene so do not forget to keep the case clean and the solution fresh. Once a week wash the case out in fresh soapy water and then rinse it thoroughly under the hot tap.

5–3 Can I See?

Sometimes your lens will displace off the centre of the eye either due to inexperienced insertion or rubbing the eye unwittingly. Re-centring the lens is an easy task even if you do not know where it has gone.

If you know where the lens is, look straight into the mirror and turn your whole head away from the side where the lens is lodged whilst still staring into the mirror (diagram 5.4) e.g. If the lens is under the lower lid, dip your chin down so

5–4 Finding the Decentred Lens

that you are looking up. The lens then becomes more
exposed. Now pull the lid back at the point where the lens
is lodged and use the lid margin as a pusher to push the lens
up onto the cornea. Take care only to apply gentle pressure
to the lens on the eyeball so that it has the best chance of
recentering easily. You may find yourself chasing the lens
around the eye at first but you will soon master the best
technique. If you cannot get it centred you will either find
that it will pop out or you can remove it with a rubber suction holder.

The most difficult lens to recentre is the one stuck in the
inner corner nearest the nose. There is no eyelid to help
push, so you have to fully turn the head and lay your index
finger across the inner corner so that when you look straight

ahead again the lens is forced to the centre (Diagram 5.5).

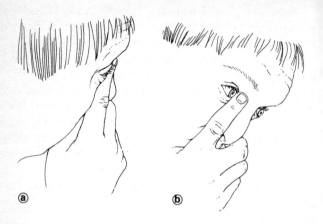

ⓐ   ⓑ

5–5 Recentring Lens from Inner Corner

If you do not know where the lens is, shut the eye concerned but keep the other eye open. Roll the eye down and try to feel for the lens through the eyelids using your thumb and fingers. Gently press your fingertips onto your eyeball through your eyelids as far out to the edge as you can. Now slowly bring them together like a tulip closing so that the lids are pinched up and pulled away from the centre of your eye. The lens should be trapped in the middle and will recentre. If this fails, look downwards and feel through the upper lid for a lens lodged at the very top of the eye. Then try to pull it down by feeling through the lid using two or three fingers.

Finally, if you cannot find it, is it actually in your eye? (See chapter 8). If it is lost up at the top you can leave it

there, even when asleep, until you can get to your practitioner next day.

When taking the lenses out, remember that lens hygiene is
as important as when putting them in. Sit at the same workstation but keep a bottle of rinsing solution handy.

Take off the right case lid and then take out the right lens
and clean it with a few drops of cleaning solution, rinse it
and place in the case and put the lid back on. Do the same
with the left lens once the right lens is safely away. If you
cannot see to clean the lenses, take them out one at a time
and put them in the temporary container. Put your spectacles on and clean the lenses one at a time before putting
each one carefully away in the main case.

There are three basic methods of lens removal and you
have to be taught the one most suitable for you by your
practitioner.

Method 1

Stare into the mirror and open your eyes really wide. Use
the index finger only pressed into the outer corner of the
eye (Diagram 5.6) and move your chin up and down whilst
rolling the finger to make the lids taut. It should be possible
to catch the lens between the lids so that when you blink it
pops out. You have to keep pulling the lids taut and then
blink. Alternatively, once the lens is caught, you can look
towards the nose so that the narrowing of the lids will force
the lens to pop out.

Method 2

If method 1 merely displaces the lens off centre, you don't
have to recentre it, you could use a suction holder to
remove it if you have one. A suction holder can be used to

5–6 One finger Lens Removal

take the lens straight from the centre. The method is much the same as when putting a lens in. The sucker is held by the thumb and index finger and touched gently onto the lens on the centre of the eye whilst holding back the lids. The lens comes away with the suction cup (Diagram 5.7). Some suckers have to be squeezed to get suction and others are solid and just have to be pressed on. All suction holders work best if the end is wetted with rinsing solution. Don't lick it!

Method 3
If you have narrow eyelids you may choose to use the two finger method (Diagram 5.8). Using the forefinger of each hand put one on the middle edge of the top lid and one on the middle edge of the bottom lid. Move the lids apart to free the lens and then press with the fingers to hold the edge

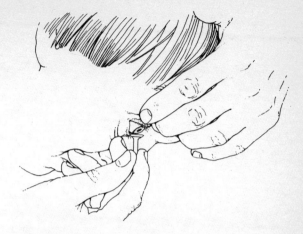

5–7 Removal with Suction Holder

of the lids against the eye. Push the lids together so that the lens flips out or just push the top lid down to force the lens to flip out over the bottom lid.

Method 3 takes careful practice and great care should be taken not to force the lens into the cornea.

Soft Lenses

The steps to follow are as follows:

After carrying out the hygiene routine, remove the right lens from the right side of the case either by tipping out the contents or by picking the lens from the dome of the case. Be careful not to fold it. Rinse the lens with saline and check that it is not inside out. This can be done by two methods. Firstly by putting the lens on the tip of your finger

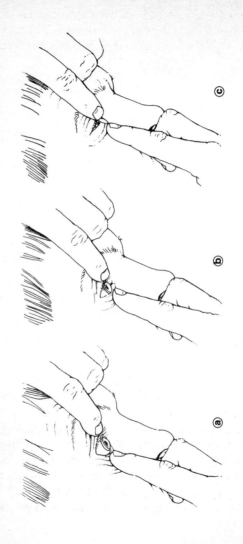

5–8 **Two Finger Method of Removal**

and examining the profile against a light background. You can see the edge turning out if it is the inside out (Diagram 5.9). Secondly the lens curls up more easily if it is the right way round.

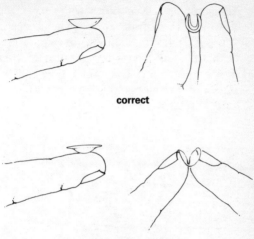

correct

incorrect (inside out)

5–9 Inside out or not

Once you are sure that the lens is correct, place it on the tip of the index finger (or any finger of your choice) after giving it a last rinse with saline. The lens will sit proud on your finger provided the lens is wet and the finger is dry. If the finger is wet the lens may flop back onto the fingertip.

Look straight ahead into the mirror, pull the lower lid down and at the same time lower the chin so that the lower half of your eye is more exposed. The lens will now be about an inch from the eye and can be gently pressed over the lower half of the eye before withdrawing the finger (Diagram 5.10). If you cannot control your blink reflex the top lid must be held firmly by the other hand. To do this bring the hand over the forehead to hold the edge of the lid with the fingertips (Diagram 5.2). Sometimes, with very thin lenses, it is helpful to pull the top lid away from the eye by the lashes and to physically close the eye over the top of the lens. Check that the lens has moved onto the centre of the eye by ensuring you can see (Diagram 5.3) by covering the left eye. If the lens does not go in at the first attempt rinse it with saline and repeat the procedure

5–10 Soft Lens Insertion

If the eye hurts when the lens is put in there may be some dust trapped under it. To correct this, place your index finger on the lens, slide it off, down and outwards and then slide it around in a circular fashion before recentring. This usually relieves the problem but if it does not, take it out and start again.

Refill the case with soaking solution or saline and replace the lid. Now you can put the left one in. You may use the same hand to insert the left lens or switch to the other hand if you prefer.

Always carry a lens case full of saline with you so that you can remove the lenses if necessary. Also take your spectacles in a crush-proof case. If you need to remove your lenses during the day, for example whilst swimming, you can store them in fresh saline until you want to put them back in. The full cleaning and storage routine only has to be done once a day.

Soft lenses rarely displace off the centre of the eye unless they become folded due to inexperienced insertion. Occasionally a lens slips up under the top lid or into the inner corner. All you have to do is pull the lid back, put your finger on the lens and slide it towards the middle. If it is folded, it will come out of the eye. Very rarely the lens will get folded and lodge right at the very top under the lid. If this happens, look as far down as you can and pull the top lid up as far as you can. Using the lid as a pusher attempt to push the lens down. If it will not come leave it and eventually it will work down on its own. You can do no harm sleeping with a decentred lens, so you can see your practitioner next day.

Taking soft lenses out. Make sure your hands are clean and that the case has fresh storage solution in it. Start by removing the right lens. Place your index finger on the lens and slide it down by moving your chin up whilst looking in the mirror (Diagram 5.11). Use the middle finger to keep the lower lid down. While your index finger is still on the

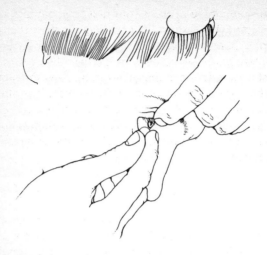

5–11 Soft Lens Removal

lens bring your thumb onto the lens surface and pinch your
forefinger and thumb together. The lens will crumple up
and come away from the eye and should be removed without unduly squeezing it. If you do squeeze it too hard so
that the lens folds and sticks to itself, place it in the temporary case in saline so that it can rehydrate for a few minutes
before you attempt to unfold it.

Now clean the lens. Place it in the palm of the left hand
and, using your index finger, rub it gently with a few drops
of cleaning solution. After twenty seconds transfer it to the
palm of the right hand and rinse it twice with saline solution
whilst gently rubbing it. Place the lens in the right side of
the case and replace the lid before starting to remove the
left lens.

If you cannot see to clean your first lens, put it in saline in the temporary case whilst your remove the other lens. Then put your glasses on so that you can clean each lens in turn before putting them away properly in the case.

Most people can take their lenses out using the method above but for the few who find it difficult there is an alternative. Use the two finger method as described under method 3 in rigid lenses (Diagram 5.8). The lens crumples up and falls out rather than flipping out. This is best done leaning over a mirror.

Scleral Lenses

These look the most daunting to put in and out but in fact they are very easy indeed. The lenses are usually stored dry so when they are removed from the case they should be rinsed under a running tap and wetting solution or saline applied before insertion. Your practitioner will explain how to identify the top of the lens.

To put a scleral lens in, hold the lens with the thumb and middle finger and rest the index finger on the middle of the lens (Diagram 5.12). Look down and pull the top lid up with the fingers of the other hand brought down over the forehead. Tilt the lens into the gap under the top lid and gently push the lens up whilst pushing the lid down over the lens but still look down. Use the top lid to hold the lens and then release the right hand to pull the lower lid down with the middle finger so that the lid pops over the edge of the lens. Look straight ahead and the lens will be in place.

Cover the other eye to check for sight (Diagram 5.3) or look in the mirror to check it is in position before starting the other one.

5–12 Holding Scleral Lens Ready for Insertion

There are two recognised methods for removing scleral lenses:

Method 1
Look down and place the middle finger on the edge of the top lid beside the nose. Press the lid and pull it upwards so that the lid catches the top edge of the lens. Keep looking down and slowly move the finger along the top edge whilst pressing against the eyeball (Diagram 5.13). The whole top edge of the lens will now be caught by the lid and by gently massaging with the same finger the lens will loose its grip on the eye and pop up and out. To encourage it to move up you should slowly stop looking down and look straight ahead.

Method 2
Using a rubber suction holder look up and place it on the

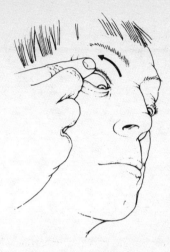

5–13 One Finger method of Scleral Removal

lower half of the lens as near to the bottom as possible (Diagram 5.14). Pull the lower lid down with your other hand. By pulling gently but firmly the lens should come out attached to the sucker.

Once out, scleral lenses are usually stored dry. Rub the lens with cleaning solution for fifteen seconds and rinse under a cold tap. The lens should then be dried with a soft cloth and placed in the case·

General Points on Looking After Lenses

When a lens is removed from the eye it should be cleaned with a surfactant cleaner and well rinsed as described above. It is important to put the lenses away clean and in the correct side of the case. The case and temporary case

5–14 Scleral Removal with Suction Holder

should also be kept clean. There are special solutions for particular types of lens and you should not muddle up the types. In particular, it is very dangerous to use hard lens solutions on soft lenses! Never change the make of solution without discussing it with your practitioner as only he knows the exact nature of your lens material, so only he is qualified to advise you.

Chapter 6
Care Systems, Solutions and Accessories

Let us first of all consider why we need a care system at all. What is wrong with tap water and spit? The correct use of solutions ensures:
1. Good contact lens comfort especially on insertion.
2. That the lens remains sterile so that it is safe for use.
3. That the lens surfaces are kept clean and free from debris and other deposits.
4. Longer lens life.
5. Minimal risk of infection and other eye problems.

When your practitioner gives you a care system to use he considers the following questions:
a) Is the system suitable for the type of material used?
b) Is there a possibility of allergic or toxic reaction?
c) Is the system effective for the job it should do?
d) Is the system easy to use?
e) Is the system readily available and affordable?
f) Is the system safe even if incorrectly used?

Let us consider the different types of solutions needed by contact lens users. You may not need all the types but it is sensible to understand how they work and why they are needed.

How Does a Wetting Solution work?
The tears in the eye are the eyes natural wetting solution. The tears, an oil and water solution, are spread over the eye by the eyelids with every blink. Stimulus to the eye, such as soap or emotion, makes these tears overflow with extra water and, as most people have found out, they taste salty.

The tears contain oils to spread the film, water to keep the eye moist, salt to stop stinging, special enzymes that kill bugs and cellular debris that the lids wipe off the surface of the eye.

When a contact lens is put onto the eye it breaks the film of tears on the surface of the eye and stops the eyelid from fully rubbing over the surface of the eye. A well-fitting contact lens will settle into the tear film so that the tear reforms across the lens and underneath the lens, sandwiched against the eye. When the eye blinks the lens moves up and down within that tear film. It does not actually press against the cornea if it is properly fitted.

It has been shown that when plastics are immersed in water they take five to ten minutes to become fully wetted. A wetting solution is a solution that coats the surface of the lens and remains on the surface, aiding quicker wetting, and thus allows the lens to settle into the tear film immediately. The wetting solution disperses after ten to fifteen minutes by which time it has done its job and the eye's natural tears take over. Wetting solutions are usually only needed for rigid lenses, as soft lenses are naturally wet.

How Does a Rewetting Solution work?
Not everybody's eyes produce sufficient tears or sufficient amounts of oils in the tears to keep the tear sandwich complete. If the lens is especially large or thick the problems are

exacerbated. The tear film then begins to break down and the cornea becomes dry. Rather than having to remove the lens to wet it again some people like to instill a rewetting solution.

One or two drops are inserted into the eye under the lower lid and the eye is blinked. The slightly less viscous solution recoats the lens while it is in the eye and immediately the eye feels more comfortable. The rewetting solution surrounds the lens and settles it back into the broken tear film.

How Does a Soaking Solution work?

In order to keep the lens hydrated it is sensible to keep it in a solution compatible with the eye but able to disinfect the lens and keep it clean. The main constituents for soaking solutions are salt and water (saline) as in the tears. Soft contact lenses contain up to 85% of their weight as water. If the lens is allowed to dry out it shrinks to a third of its original size so a soaking solution has the function of keeping it soft. Gas permeable hard lenses may absorb up to 3% of their weight as water so they, too, need a soaking solution to maintain their correct shape.

Within the soaking solutions are three important ingredients: a bug killer, a dilute cleaning agent and a preservative. A soaking solution is therefore more than just a sterile solution. It cleans and wets the lens as well as maintaining the lens mass. The percentage of water absorbed by a soft lens is called the material's water content, hence one has the expressions 'high water content' and 'low water content'.

It is very important for soft lens wearers to change the soaking solution daily as the soft lenses absorb the soaking solution and use up much of the preservative within the solution. If the soft lens is continuously put into the same solution it will become contaminated and a serious risk of eye infection ensues.

It is even important to change the solution daily for rigid lenses even though hard lenses do not absorb the solution in the same way.

How Does a Cleaning Solution work?

One could imagine that, provided a lens is stored in a good soaking solution and wetted with a good wetting solution, then cleaning the lens would be unnecessary. With rigid lenses very often you would be right but it is a risk that should not be taken.

As lenses age they become scratched, or stubborn deposits build up. The surface cannot be relied upon to stay clean unless a cleaning solution is used. A cleaning solution is a special detergent that cleans the surface of the lens. This gives rise to the official name, 'surfactant cleaner'.

When using a surfactant cleaner, always ensure that you squirt some saline on the lens before starting the cleaning process. A lens should be cleaned with surfactant on removal from the eye NOT just before they are put in! It is a gentle rubbing action that is responsible for most of the cleaning activity with a surfactant.

Periodic cleaners are those that are used occasionally rather than every night. This category includes cleaners known as 'enzyme cleaners'. Enzymes are used to break down the proteins into acids and debris which is dissolved from the surface into the surrounding solution.

Oxidising systems, used to sterilise lenses, may also have some cleaning effect. The theory is that they break down hardened minerals such as carbonates and phosphates so that they dissolve into the surrounding water. One must remember that hydrogen peroxide systems need a neutralising agent to be used afterwards otherwise the eye may get an uncomfortable reaction. The advantage of oxidising systems is that no preservatives need be used thus reducing the chances of allergic or toxic reactions. Chlorine release tablets do not need a neutraliser.

How Does a Rinsing Solution work?

A rinsing solution is usually just a tear substitute such as saline. Unpreserved saline may be in unit dose tubes, sachets or aerosol cans. Large bottles of saline contain preservatives that may upset some eyes.

A rinsing solution is used to thoroughly rinse away other solutions from the surface of the lens e.g. after cleaning or soaking. It may also be used to rinse out the case before fresh solution is inserted.

How Does an Eye Drop work?

An eye drop is a solution that actually has an effect on the surface of the eye and is absorbed into the eye. They usually contain medicines that cure eye infections or allergies. They are usually prescribed by doctors or ophthalmologists although your U.K. optometrist may be able to prescribe them in an emergency. The optometrist may often use them in the consulting room to prevent infection, to dilate your pupils, or to anaesthetize your eye. One has to be sure that any eye drop used does not contain a preservative that is incompatable with your contact lens.

How Does an Eye Wash work?

An eye wash is a solution that can be flushed over the eye

Product Information Form

Lens Material:

Purpose

Rinsing before insertion:

Wetting solution:

Rewetting solution:

Cleaning solution:

Rinsing solution
before storage:

Soaking solution:

Oxidising solution:

Neutralising solution:

Periodic cleaner:

Eye wash:

Important Accessories:

Name of Product   *Notes*

to wash the surface and remove debris. It obviously must contain mainly saline and may be used either from tubes, sachets or inserted with an eye bath. Contact lens wearers are usually encouraged to use a few drops of unpreserved saline or an eye bath. This avoids weakening the tear layers or risking a reaction against preservatives which may be present in the eye wash.

Product Information Form

I have devised a form for you or your practitioner to fill in when you collect your new lenses. I have left lots of space. As you wear your lenses, it may need to be updated. You may not need something from every category on the form so do not be disappointed if you cannot have some of everything! I have also left a space for you to make notes about frequency of use or costs. Remember that this is personal to you and does not necessarily apply to somebody else even with the same lens material.

Cases and Accessories

There are all sorts of accessories available for contact lens wearers. Let us look at the merits of these.

1. Heat Disinfection Units

Heat disinfection units heat the case containing soft lenses in saline to a temperature of approximately 80 degrees Celsius for about thirty minutes. In short, they pasteurize the lenses rather than sterilise them. The bugs on the lenses and in the solution are killed but spores remain. Unless the pasteurizing takes place daily the lenses quickly grow new bugs and fungi.

Together with heat units came the need for cheap saline solutions. People used to make up saline using salt tablets and purified water. Bugs in the purified water were killed by the boiler. It has now been shown that there is a very real risk of serious amoeba infection from home made saline especially if it is used for rinsing rather than boiling. Today you are advised to buy safe, unpreserved saline in aerosol cans, tubes or sachets.

2.   Heat units with Ultra-Sonic Cleaning Devices
Some heat units these days incorporate ultra-sonic agitation that shakes the surface deposits from the lenses. The manufacturers claim a great saving on both storage solutions and cleaners.

3.   Sponges
Special sponges have been designed to aid surface cleaning of lenses. The sponge is soaked with saline and surfactant. The lens is placed on the end of the finger and rubbed gently over the surface of the sponge. The abrasive action cleans off surface deposits. The system works well for soft lenses provided you are careful, and will clean the outer surface of rigid lenses.

4.   Suction Holders
There are several types of suction holder available. They may be either big or little, or, squeezy or solid. The big suckers are for scleral lenses and the little ones are for rigid corneal lenses. The solid suckers, once wetted, will stick to any smooth surface, even your eye! They have to be handled carefully so get some advice from your practitioner before using any suction holder. Some solid suckers have

angled heads so that your hand does not have to go in front of the mirror blocking your view of the lens. Squeezy suckers have to be squeezed to expel air and when you stop squeezing they will suck onto the lens. They are safer for the novice. There is one squeezy sucker that will work on some types of soft lens.

5.   Special Removers

There are two different rubber devices that can be used to aid soft lens removal. Both act like soft tweezers and should only be used if advised by your practitioner.

6.   Devices for the hard of seeing

Some people are unable to see what they are doing when inserting and removing their lenses and various devices have been made to help.

One of the earliest ones is to use a small penlight and to put a dismembered hollow section holder on the end. The lens can be balanced on the sucker and by looking at the light it can be guided into place.

Scleral lens users may have special notches on the side of the lens so that they can feel which lens is which and which way round they should be.

Some people have to have special make-up spectacles which have each lens on a hinge so that you look with one eye whilst placing the contact lens into the other. Then you hinge up the other lens and drop down a close up lens in front of the contact lens wearing eye so that you can see to put the second lens in.

There are special mirrors available that give extra high magnification and they may also have an internal light to brighten the view.

Chapter 7
Wearing times and aftercare

Wearing Times

When you first get lenses it is important to allow your eyes to adapt to them. However permeable your lenses are, your eyes still need time to adapt to contact lenses. Also the eyelids, which are responsible for keeping dust out of the eyes and spreading tears over the cornea, have to get used to the lens's presence.

Each type of lens has a safe adaptation period. You could go faster but you run the risk of rejection. If you follow the suggestions made in table 7.1 you should not go far wrong. You must, however, follow the advice of your practitioner who may give you totally different wearing times and after-care (A.C.) appointments because he knows your eyes and your lenses. I have left a spare column for you to fill in his recommendations if they are different from mine.

It is possible to divide your wearing time into two if you wish but this will, of course, involve putting your lenses in and out twice. The dates where aftercare visits are needed is also an individual requirement.

Aftercare Visits

I have already talked about aftercare visits in chapter 4 but

Table 7.1: Suggested Maximum Wearing Time in Hours.
N.B. Follow your practitioner's advice

LENS TYPE:	SCLERAL	CORNEAL HARD	LOW G.P.	HIGH G.P.	SOFT	OTHER INSTRUC- TIONS
Day 1	1	3	3	3	5	
Day 2	1.5	3.5	3.5	4	6	
Day 3	2	4	4	5	7	
Day 4	2.5	4.5	4.5	6	8	
Day 5	3	5	5	7	9	
Day 6	3.5	5.5	5.5	8	10	
Day 7	4	6	6	9	11	
	1st AC appt			1st AC appt	1st AC appt	
Day 8	4.5	6.5	6.5	10	12	
Day 9	5	7	7	11	13	
Day 10	5.5	7.5	7.5	12	14	
Day 11	6	8	8	13	15	
Day 12	6.5	8	8.5	14	15+	
Day 13	7	8	9	15	15+	
Day 14	7.5	8	9.5	15+	15+	
		1st AC appt	1st AC appt			
Day 15	8	8.5	10	15+	15+	
Day 16	8.5	9	10.5	15+	15+	
Day 17	9	9.5	11	15+	15+	
	2nd AC appt					
Day 18	A	10	11.5	15+	15+	
Day 19	S	10.5	12	15+	15+	
Day 20		11	12.5	15+	15+	
Day 21	A	11.5	13	15+	15+	

Day 22	D	12	13.5	15+	15+
Day 23	V	12.5	14	15+	15+
Day 24	I	13	14.5	15+	15+
Day 25	S	13.5	15	15+	15+
Day 26	E	14	15+	15+	15+
Day 27	D	14	15+	15+	15+
Day 28		14	15+	15+	15+
		2nd AC appt	2nd AC appt	2nd AC appt	2nd AC appt

this was in connection with the average costs involved. By the time you reach the one month stage (See Table 7.1) you will have had two aftercare visits. You will now need to see your practitioner at regular intervals to ensure that your eyes can safely continue to wear the lenses prescribed and the lenses are not deteriorating in any way.

After Day 28 you will need to see your practitioner after a further 6 weeks and a further 3 months. You will also need to see him if any problems arise.

At the 6 months stage *you should plan to have regular aftercare for ever.* Generalising, you should see your practitioner as follows:

Soft extended wear   *6 monthly*
Soft daily wear   *9 monthly*
High gas permeable   *9 months – 1 year*
Low gas permeable   *yearly*
Corneal hard   *yearly*
Scleral   *yearly*

By visiting your practitioner regularly long term success is more likely to be assured. However, neglect of aftercare is probably the biggest single cause of long term problems with contact lenses. If a problem is spotted early on it can be dealt with. If it remains untreated for years then damage could be done to the eye.

What to Do if Wearing Time Is Disrupted

Several things could happen to disrupt your wearing schedule either at an early stage or once you are fully adapted. For example:

1. You might get flu or some other illness.
2. You might lose a lens.
3. You might go away unexpectedly and not risk taking your lenses.
4. You might have an eye infection.

What should you do? If you have had an eye infection, you should return your lenses to your practitioner to be sterilised and, ideally, you should be checked over before you resume lens wear.

Seek advice from your practitioner about rebuilding your time. Otherwise, the rule is **for every day you have not worn your lenses, reduce your wearing time by one hour and build up again**. So, if you are a hard lens wearer and you have reached 12 hours wear and you have left your lenses out for four days, return to 8 hours wear and build up by half an hour per day.

How to Cope with Hot, Smoky Atmospheres

When you are building up wearing time, particularly with hard lenses, you may find your eyes upset by hot, smoky atmospheres. If you cannot avoid such atmospheres then the rule to follow is **one hour in the hot, smoky atmosphere is equivalent to three hours in the fresh air.** So for every hour in a smoky atmosphere reduce your wearing time by two hours.

Corneal hard lens wearers particularly should beware of overwearing their lenses in the early stages. If you go too fast and your cornea does not adapt quickly enough you could get an overwear reaction otherwise known as 'The 3 a.m. Syndrome'. Several hours after you have removed your lenses the cornea becomes highly sensitive and painful so that you actually wake up with the pain. It is almost impossible to open your eyes and often the only cure is to stay in a darkened room for 24 hours whilst you recover. Even long-term wearers can get this reaction if they stay out late at a smokey party, so, if you know you are going to be out late either put your lenses in later in the day or take them out for a two hour rest before you go out. Nobody should get the 3.a.m. syndrome if they are sensible.

What Sort of Problems Could Arise?
Every type of lens seems to have its own particular problems either because of the lens or because of the care system used. Some eyes are far more sensitive and quicker to react than others. Here are a few things to look out for all of which should be reported back to your practitioner:

1. Misty, hazy vision at the end of the wearing time. It is very common to see a fog after removing hard lenses and it indicates that the cornea has swollen. You should make a note of how long it takes to regain clear vision with your spectacles. Anything beyond thirty minutes should be

reported urgently to your practitioner.

2. Red eyes after wearing the lenses could be a normal reaction but usually it is a sign of lack of oxygen.

3. Red eyes before you put the lenses in combined with yellow mucous in the corners is typical of an eye infection and should be treated by your doctor. You should consult your practitioner before resuming contact lens wear.

4. White spot on the cornea combined with some redness. This is likely to be a corneal ulcer and you should see your practitioner who will refer you to your General Practitioner once he has checked the symptoms. **Stop wearing your lenses immediately.**

5. Frequent red eye reactions could be caused by unsuitable lenses or by a toxic reaction to one of the solutions used. Consult your practitioner for advice because you might be doing something wrong.

6. Soft lenses keep sliding up under the top lid and the lenses are covered in protein. This unusual reaction occurs with a particular type of allergic conjunctivitis that causes bumps to form under the eyelids and protein to deposit on the lenses. Apart from mild itching there is often no pain. Treatment is needed to reduce the size of the bumps and a different type of lens may be needed.

7. Very poor spectacle vision after wearing lenses. This usually occurs after wearing hard lenses for many years and is due to the cornea becoming distorted. It should not be confused with the spectacle blur that occurs when adapting to lenses. The cure is usually to refit with higher gas-permeable rigid lenses or even soft lenses. The cornea will then

straighten up again. Very often this occurs as the eyes get drier with age or with hormonal changes.

Sometimes people decide to give up contact lenses and revert to spectacles. This can be very traumatic if the cornea is distorted so the practitioner will often refit with gas permeable lenses (which are much more commonly prescribed than hard lenses) to allow good vision whilst the eye undistorts. Spectacles will gradually become clearer over a period of several months.

Because spectacles are usually a poorer optical system than contact lenses it can be quite difficult to get used to them after wearing contact lenses for years. It is therefore sensible to wear your spectacles for a few hours every week to keep your eyes in tune with them. It is also sensible to keep your spectacles up to date.

Serious Problems

Serious problems are very rarely caused by contact lenses, but contact lenses can be an added complication to serious eye conditions. For example all eyes are susceptible to eye infections (See chapter 11).

There are three rare problems particularly associated with contact lens wearers.

1. Infection from old purified water. Until recently, it was common for people to mix purified water and salt tablets to make up saline. It has been shown that a particular bug called the Acanthamoeba thrives in this liquid and can lead to a very serious infection that if not treated promptly and properly could cause severe visual loss. It is therefore important to use sterile saline.

2. Severe corneal ulcer can be caused by the cold sore virus (Herpes Simplex). If the virus gets into the cornea through an abrasion it can cause a very painful condition and if not treated promptly can lead to visual loss. It is therefore important **never to lick your lenses**.

3. Blood vessel infiltration from the edge of the eye. Blood vessels will grow into the cornea in response to long term oxygen starvation or dryness of the cornea. It is caused by a combination of lens pressure and lack of oxygen and can be prevented, or its effects limited, by regular aftercare check-ups.

It is important to stress that these problems can occur with any type of lens but **they are rare**. Curiously, soft lens wearers are at the greatest risk because the lens bandages the eye so that pain is not obvious when problems are occurring. Figures from eye hospitals suggest that the incidence of serious damage to the eye from contact lenses is about 1 in 100,000. Obviously it pays to be careful and if you are worried by any suspicious symptoms consult your practitioner urgently.

Chapter 8
Finding a lost lens

The most popular time to mislay a contact lens is when you are putting it in or taking it out, especially when you are a beginner. If it does go missing then the first thing to realise is 'it cannot have gone far!' Ask yourself the question 'Is it in my eye?' People spend endless hours searching for a lost lens on the floor when in fact it was tucked up under the top eyelid. The last thing to tell yourself is 'Don't Panic!'

The way to find a lens is as follows:
1. Check the lens is not in your eye.
2. Check the workstation surfaces.
3. Check the mirror and the case.
4. Check it is not stuck to a solution bottle or your hair.
5. Maybe it is on the floor. If so, it is probably near your feet so it is important not to step on it. Take your feet out of your shoes and gently step backwards as far as you can go. If you are on a chair step out to the side. Shake your clothing gently and watch for the lens to fall. Is it in your lap, in a turnup or pocket? Turn the lights up and carefully search the floor and any ledges it may have caught on. Look from all angles and use a torch to illuminate any shaded areas.

If you have not found it by now check again that it is not

in your eye go through the recentering procedures described in chapter 5. You will do yourself no harm sleeping with a displaced lens in your eye. If you are worried that it may still be in your eye go to see your practitioner immediately or the next day. He will find it easily if it is there.

Lost soft lenses

When a soft lens is lost out of solution it dries up. Depending on its water content, a soft lens could become one third of its normal size, rather opaque and wrinkly around the edges. It no longer looks like or feels like a soft lens after twenty minutes or so. It also becomes brittle so, if you do find it, be careful not to break it picking it up. If it is stuck to a surface rewet it with saline for a few minutes where it lies. It will absorb the water and become soft and pliable again. Once it is safely recovered, pop it in saline solution for at least thirty minutes before going through the normal sterilising procedures. Whatever you do do not put it straight into your eye without cleaning it, checking it for damage and resoaking it. If in doubt let your practitioner check it over for you.

Finding a hard lens

If all else fails you can sometimes find a rigid lens by using the suction pipe of a vaccuum cleaner with a stocking stretched over the end. The lens will be trapped on the stocking and will not get sucked into the machine. This method could also work with a soft lens if it is not stuck down.

Down the drain

It is amazing how often a lens goes down the drain. They either get lost while rinsing a rigid lens under the tap without the plug in or the conscientious owner rinses out the case under the hot tap but forgets that the lenses are (were) in there. I have heard tales of people rushing to the outside drain with a colander and then running the tap until the lens is flushed through. The second method, especially if you live in a flat with internal drains, is to dismantle the U-bend under the sink before running the tap again. Provided you stop yourself in time and turn the tap off you may be lucky enough to retrieve the lens. Once retrieved the lens should be inspected for damage, cleaned and resoaked before wear. A soft lens may need to be returned to the practitioner for professional cleaning. You can get special sink sieves from your practitioner to avoid this happening. They are not very hygienic things because they catch most things going through but they do allow a margin of safety if you are an accident-prone person.

In the swimming pool

If you lose a lens in a swimming pool you have two choices.
1. Offer prizes to macho young men to find it for you.
2. Search the filtration system daily to see if it gets caught.

If it is a soft lens forget it. If not quickly found the chemicals in the pool will not do it any good even if you are lucky enough to find it. A rigid lens will be quite usable after a soak.

Swallowed!

It is not uncommon for lenses to be swallowed. The scenario is usually 'I took my lenses out and not having my case handy I put them in a glass of water beside my bed. During the night my partner got thirsty and drank them!'

If they are soft lenses forget it. They would be digested. Rigid lenses can be found if you are very patient and very desperate not to pay for new ones. The method of searching for the lenses is not recommended by the author! The lenses, when found, should be thoroughly cleaned and disinfected before re-use.

General points
Always follow a sensible routine, ideally at the same workstation, when inserting and removing your lenses. Always spread out a white cloth or hankerchief at other times. Never take lenses out in poorly lit conditions. Always put the plug in where sinks are involved. Never take the lenses out in the wind or whilst in a swimming pool or bath. Carry a spare case with you at all times. If you use your commonsense at all times you should never lose a lens.

Please refer to chapter 12 for information on insuring your lenses and practitioners' replacement schemes.

Chapter 9
Making up with Contact Lenses

There was a time when the average male would not have felt the need to read this chapter. However, I would recommend that all contact lens wearers browse through it as there is more to make-up than meets the eye! It is very important to avoid lens contamination and eye problems caused by cosmetics, soaps and creams.

Choosing Your Make-Up
It is sensible to avoid cheap or unknown brands though there are stringent tests that have to be passed before cosmetics can be marketed. It is best to choose brands that are specially formulated for contact lens wearers. Hypoallergenic make-ups specifically omit known irritants. There are several makes available and your practitioner should be able to advise you which are available in your locality.

Washing Your Hands
Do not wash your hands with antiseptic or deodorant soaps before handling your lenses. The hexachlorophene that they contain will cling to the skin even after rinsing and will cause a stinging sensation if it gets into your eye. You should

use unperfumed or simple soap. Also try to air dry your hands or use a towel that does not leave dust on your hands.

Creams

Avoid getting face creams or oils into your eyes. They could remain there overnight and cause trouble when the lenses are inserted. Wearers of extended wear lenses should be extra careful not to cloud their lenses! If you have to use such products apply them lightly using a cotton wool bud near the edge of the lids. Oil-free make-up removers are preferable.

Hand creams often contain silicones, so do highly gas-permeable contact lenses. The two have an affinity. One of the most common reasons for gas-permeable lenses to grease up continuously is contamination with hand cream. If you use hand creams, use them sparingly and preferably *after* you have handled your lenses. The best advice is to avoid them altogether.

Face Powder

When you use face powder make sure you have your eyes shut and try not to spread it around the eyes. Also be careful not to cloud the atmosphere more than you have to. If it gets on the eyelids or lashes remove the excess powder with a damp tissue.

Hairspray

Not only will hairspray irritate your eyes but it will stick to the surface of a contact lens. This will lead to clouding of the lens and irritation. It is possible to polish it off rigid lenses but it may permanently damage soft lenses. It is for this reason that you should not wear lenses at a beauty salon.

If you need to use a hairspray, shut your eyes, spray and walk out of the area before you open them again. Also do not spray it near other people. They may have lenses in too.

Applying Eye Make-up

As a general rule it is best to put your lenses in before you put your make-up on. This is because most people see better with their lenses in, there is less chance of soiling them and you will not upset your make-up when putting the lenses in.

When applying base and eye shadow to the top lid tilt your chin up and look slightly down into the mirror. If your skin is dry the base and eye shadow may go on more smoothly if you use a non- greasy moisturising lotion first.

If you find it easier to put your lenses in after making up be sure to wash your hands very thoroughly before touching the lenses.

Eye-Shadow

Avoid powdered or glittery eye shadows as they may contaminate the contact lenses and irritate the eye. There are several makes of eyeshadow specially formulated for contact lens wearers.

Mascara

It is essential to use only water-soluble mascara because if it gets into your eye it will just dissolve. Admittedly it can run if you cry but the insoluble flaky types may get under the lens and scratch your eye.

In particular, do not use chunky mascara that adds length to the lashes. This type contains tiny bits of hair which can drop into the eye and cause intense irritation.

Apply mascara sparingly and blot with a tissue from beneath the lashes. Use the same blotting technique to avoid the mascara spreading if your eyes water.

Eye Liner

You should never apply eye liner to the inner edge of the lid between the lashes and the eye. Inevitably it will get into your tear film and also it will block your tear and mucous glands. Eye liners should be water-soluble and should not flake.

Make-Up Remover

It is usually best to take your lenses out and put them away before removing your make-up. This is, of course, not practicable with extended wear lenses.

Provided water-soluble products have been used you should be able to use a warm flannel to remove the make-up. Alternatively, splash your closed eyes with warm water and use tissues to remove it. If you have to use a make-up remover use it sparingly and remember to keep the use of creams to a minimum.

Cotton wool buds can be very useful for getting into awkward creases because they absorb the make-up and the remover and therefore avoid spreading it.

Chapter 10
Special types of Contact Lenses

Special types of contact lenses have been developed to overcome unusual sight defects.

1.   LENSES FOR ASTIGMATISM

Astigmatism is no great problem if it is due to the cornea being distorted because the liquid trapped between the rigid contact lens and the eye helps to correct the astigmatism. However sometimes it is due to other factors. **Irregular Astigmatism** is where the cornea is not evenly distorted, the degree of distortion varies across the surface. **Mixed Astigmatism** occurs where the cornea is distorted and also another surface within the eye is distorted too. **Lenticular Astigmatism** is where the cornea is not distorted but the crystalline lens within the eye is distorted (rare).

Because there are various types of astigmatism your practitioner may find that when the contact lens is put on the eye some of the astigmatism is not corrected and therefore the sight is not as good as it could be. The amount uncorrected is called the **Residual Astigmatism**.

Back Surface Toric

If the cornea is very astigmatic a spherical contact lens does not fit properly but rocks on the eye. A special lens with a distorted back surface has to be tailor made to fit the cornea. This is called a back surface toric.

Bi-Toric

Sometimes a good back surface toric fit leaves some astigmatism uncorrected and the correction for this residual astigmatism has to be ground onto the front surface of the lens. This is called a bi-toric and is difficult to make and sometimes difficult to wear.

Front Surface Toric

In the majority of cases correcting the residual astigmatism is achieved by grinding the front surface of the lens. Methods then have to be employed to stop the lens from turning out of position. The methods used are as follows:

(a) Weighting

The lens is made thin at the top and thick at the bottom. This is called prism ballast. This ensured that the astigmatic correction stays in the correct position.

(b) Inferior Truncation

After weighting the lens it is often necessary to cut off the bottom edge of the lens. By squaring off the bottom, the lens edge will align with the lower eyelid and this will stop it from rocking. Inferior Truncation with Prism Ballast is the most popular method of stabilising front surface toric rigid and soft lenses (Diagram 10.1).

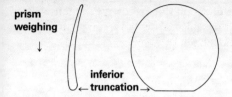

prism weighing

↓

inferior
← **truncation** →

10–1 Weighting and Truncation

(c) Double Truncation
Sometimes in order to avoid weighting a lens it is possible to square off the top and bottom of the lens. The lens then has an even thickness and tends to align either way up between the eyelids (Diagram 10.2).

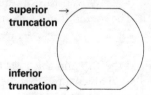

superior →
truncation

inferior
truncation →

10–2 Double Truncation

(d) Stabilisation Zones
A variation of double truncation is to thin the top and bottom of the lenses whilst leavng the horizontal area relatively fat. The lids will tend to hold the lens in position. This

method is used almost exclusively with large soft lenses (Diagram 10.3).

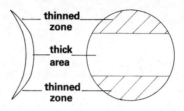

10–3 Stabilisation Zones

(e) Vents
Sometimes the back of the lens has a little groove or vent that allows tears to get behind the lens at the fattest point. This is usually at the bottom of a prism ballasted, truncated lens.

2.   Bifocal Lenses

Between forty and fifty years of age people develop the condition called 'Presbyopia' (see Chapter 1). Often they have had good sight all their lives and only now become dependent on spectacles. Contact lens wearers are faced with the prospect of putting on reading spectacles. Existing spectacle wearers are faced with the prospect of two pairs of glasses which they must take on and off in order to read and see in the distance or bifocal glasses.

Age is no barrier to wearing contact lenses so if you have not tried before there is no reason why you should not try now. Bifocal contact lenses can be more versatile than bifocal glasses.

There are two basic methods of giving bifocal vision. The lens has to have two separate strengths, one for distance and one for reading.

Alternating (Translating – USA) Bifocal

This lens is a bit like a bifocal spectacle lens. It has a portion towards the bottom of the lens called a reading segment. The main part of the lens is for distance. The lens is weighted (Prism Ballast) and squared off at the bottom (Truncated).

When you look down, the lens is pushed up by the lower lid so that the reading segment moves over the pupil (See Diagram 10.5). When you look up again the lens drops down and the distance portion covers the pupil (Diagram 10.4). As a result, you are not aware of the reading portion when you are walking along. The vision alternates between distance and reading as you look down. In order to get full coverage of the pupil this method works best if you have small pupils. Pupils tend to get smaller as you get older.

This design is best made in the corneal hard lens material, Perspex, because the reading segment is fused into the plastic but similar designs are being developed in gas permeable and soft lenses with limited success.

Concentric Bifocals

The most recent lenses to be developed utilize this method. This design can be used for all materials but may be difficult to manufacture.

The idea is that there is a main lens with a tiny, round,

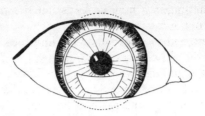

10–4 Bifocal Looking at Distance

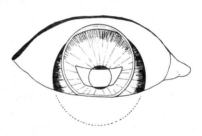

10–5 Bifocal Looking to Read

central portion with a different strength. This segment may be focused for distance or reading and sits within the pupil area all the time so that the eye always sees both pictures, distance and reading, simultaneously. Now it is up to the brain to concentrate on the picture it wants to see.

The brain is quite used to doing this already. Try a little experiment. Hold your finger up 10 inches in front of your nose while you are looking at the television. You will notice that the television picture is clear whilst your finger is hopelessly out of focus and double.

Now, assuming that your eyes are able, look at your

finger. Your finger is now in focus but the television is hopelessly out of focus.

Your brain will concentrate on the image that you need and ignore the out of focus one.

It takes two or three weeks to get used to wearing a concentric bifocal. Not everybody can tolerate them but your practitioner will be able to form an opinion about your likely success at the first visit.

This method works best if you have large pupils because there is more room for the segment to share the pupil with the main lens (Diagram 10.6a).

The pupil size varies with the amount of light entering the

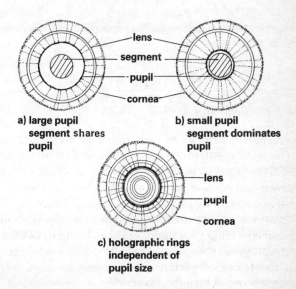

a) large pupil
   segment shares
   pupil

b) small pupil
   segment dominates
   pupil

c) holographic rings
   independent of
   pupil size

10–6 Effect of pupil size on Concentric lens

eye. When the light is bright, sunglasses help to keep the pupil open. When you focus to read the pupil gets smaller, especially if you use a good strong light (Diagram 10.6b).

The holographic (defractive) lens (Diagram 10.6c) has concentric rings of reading focus interspaced with rings of distance focus. The two focuses that result may overcome the problems of varying pupil size.

3.   COSMETIC LENSES

One can argue that all contact lenses are cosmetic. They improve the appearance! However, this expression is one given to coloured lenses that change the appearance of the eyes. This type of lens may be used either to camouflage a damaged eye or just because it is fun to change the colour of your eyes.

There are three ways to colour lenses by using either a transparent tint or solid paint.

(a) Transparent Tinting

In theory a lens can be tinted any colour you like. In practice though lenses are usually tinted in various densities of the following colours:
Grey, Blue, Green, Brown, Turquoise, Red, Yellow.

Rigid corneal lenses are normally manufactured using a pale tint so that you can see the lens more easily. A rigid corneal lens only covers part of the cornea so it does not change the colour of all the iris. It is usually soft lenses that have a noticeable cosmetic effect.

A soft lens is tinted by dyeing after it is made while the tint is already present in the material from which the rigid lens is made. Soft lenses, therefore, do not have to be tinted all over (Diagram 10.7). Usually a soft lens is tinted only in the area covering the iris.

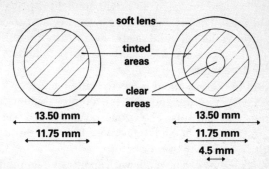

soft lens

tinted areas

clear areas

13.50 mm   13.50 mm

11.75 mm   11.75 mm

4.5 mm

10–7 Tinted areas of Soft Lens

(b) Solid Painted

This type of lens is used to cover a scarred or disfigured eye.

Soft lenses have a laminate of painted plastic sandwiched between two soft layers. The lenses are thicker than usual and not very water permeable so they may have a tendency to get a bit dry. They are not suitable for normal use as the sideways sight is blinkered.

Painted scleral lenses (see Chapter 2) are the most realistic way of totally changing the appearance of a damaged, squinting eye.

(c)

There are ways of combining transparent tinting with a translucent or opaque backing to change the colour of the normal eye just for fun.

4.   ULTRA-VIOLET INHIBITORS

Research proves that excessive ultra-violet light ages the eye early and leads to reduced vision later in life. Ultra-violet light is more prevalent in bright sunlight especially at high altitudes. The crystalline lens in the eye absorbs most of the ultra-violet light and the retina absorbs the rest. It is argued that excessive U-V leads to early cataracts and macular degeneration.

To add to the argument it has recently been shown that the ozone layer around the earth is becoming thinner due to pollution and aerosols. The ozone layer absorbs some of the harmful radiation and today more U-V gets through to the earth's surface than ever before.

Contact lenses can be made with an ultra-violet inhibitor either in soft or rigid lenses. There is no doubt that it is a good idea but it does add to the cost of lenses and considerably restricts the choice. So if the lens you need is available with an U-V inhibitor you might as well have the protection. However, you can get the same protection from a good pair of sunglasses on sunny days.

5.   ASPHERIC DESIGNS

There are special methods of shaping the back surface of a contact lens to vary the focus across the surface. This may allow some automatic correction of astigmatism and presbyopia especially with soft lens designs.

6.   SOFT-HARD LENSES

Recently lenses have been designed with a rigid lens set into a soft surround or by combining the plastics to produce a soft flange. Such lenses will correct astigmatism better than soft lenses.

7. SILICONE RUBBER LENSES

This material requires no water to maintain its mass yet it is soft and pliable. It has not yet been refined enough to be used as a successful contact lens because the material repels water and does not wet well. However this problem could soon be resolved.

Chapter 11
What to do in an emergency

There are four types of emergency that occur with contact lens wearers.
1. Loss of Lens.
2. Loss of Sight.
3. Sudden Red Eye Reaction.
4. Sudden Extreme Pain.

Obviously the right thing to do in all cases is to ring your practitioner for advice but he may not be available when needed so here are some guidelines to help you.

Loss of Lens

The best person to replace a lost lens is the practitioner who originally fitted it. He is in charge of your eyes and so he is the best person to take responsibility for supplying the new lens.

Whilst you are waiting for the new lens you may be able to continue with just one lens or you may have to revert to spectacles so it is important to keep your spectacles up to date and to carry them with you when travelling. It is important to wear your spectacles for a few hours every week to keep your eyes adapted to them. Some people who travel a lot like to take a spare set of lenses with them just in case.

Loss of Sight

If you suddenly lose your sight in one eye check the following:

(a) Is the lens still over the cornea?

(b) Are the lenses in the correct eyes?

(c) Hold the offending lens up to the light to see if it is whole and still transparent.

(d) Can you see properly through the affected eye with your spectacles on.

If you conclude that the lens is at fault but your sight is still O.K. either book an appointment to see your your practitioner or order a new lens. If you conclude that your actual sight has gone then you should see your practitioner immediately.

The two most common causes of loss of sight in one eye only are retinal detachment and retinal haemorrhage so it is nothing to do with the contact lens and must be diagnosed immediately. If your practitioner is unavailable present yourself to your general practitioner or to your nearest hospital offering an accident and emergency department. Nobody will rebuke you for wasting their time but they will be very upset for you if treatable eye disease is neglected and permanent sight loss results.

Sudden Red Eye Reaction.

There are numerous possible causes of acute red eye. Some contact lens wearers often get slightly red eyes which can be dealt with at routine visits but if you get a sudden bright red eye you should not ignore it. The rules to follow are:

(a) Take the lens out.

(b) Phone your practitioner.

(c) See your practitioner or G.P. the same day.

The cause may be anything from a damaged lens to a nasty eye infection. Once you have taken the lens out the red eye should subside but if it does not and you cannot get to see your practitioner or G.P. then it is sensible to present yourself to the accident and emergency department of your local hospital.

Remember that if you get a red eye from an infection, you should not wear the lens again until you have taken your practitioner's advice.

Sudden Extreme Pain

If your eye suddenly becomes extremely painful it could be due to dust or grit under the lens. Hold your eye open for a minute and let the tears wash it out. If it does not go away take the lens out. If you cannot get the grit out consult your practitioner urgently (or the nearest eye hospital). Avoid taking lenses out on windy corners in case they blow away.

If you get extreme pain after removing the lenses then it could be what is known as 'the overwear reaction' (see Chapter 7, Smoky atmospheres). It is not necessary to rush to your practitioner immediately but he will need to examine your eyes before you put your lenses back in.

There are four eye conditions that commonly cause extreme pain in one eye only:
(a) Keratitis (inflammation of the cornea).
(b) Iritis (inflammation of the iris).
(c) Scleritis (inflammation of the sclera).
(d) Acute Glaucoma (raised eye pressure).
All of these need urgent treatment so if you have a severe pain which is not apparently due to your lens see your practitioner, G.P. or Ophthalmologist immediately. **If in doubt – consult.**

Travelling Abroad.

If you are going abroad or moving a long way from your practitioner, ask him for a potted version of your eye details to carry with you. The following list of names and addresses are the headquarters of optometric or optical organisations in countries throughout the world. The list is by no means complete and should only be used if your practitioner is unable to recommend somebody suitable in your new locality.

AUSTRALIA.
Australian Optometrical Association
Dublin Terrace,
204, Drummond Street,
Carlton,
Victoria, 3053.
Tel. (03) 663 0063.

AUSTRIA.
Bundesinnung der Optiker
Postfach 352,
Weidner Hauptstrasse 63,
A – 1045 Wien.
Tel. (0222) 65 05/DW 3245.

CANADA.
Canadian Association of Optometrists
Suite 301,
1785, Alta Vista Drive,
Ottawa,
Ontario, K1G 3Y6.
Tel. (613) 738 4400

CYPRUS.
The Cyprus Association of Ophthalmic
Opticians
PO Box 523,
Nicosia.
Tel. 75903.

DENMARK.	Danmarks Optikerforening Kongevejs – Centret 2, DK – 2970 Hoersholm. Tel. 02 861 533.
FIJI.	Fiji Optometric Association GPO Box 537, Suva. Tel. 23433.
FRANCE.	Union Nationale des Syndicats d'Opticiens de France 45 rue de Lancry, F – 75010 Paris. Tel. 206 07 31.
GERMAN FEDERAL REPUBLIC.	W.V.A.O. Adam – Karillonstrasse 32, D – 6500 Mainz. Tel. 06131 63061.
HONG KONG.	Hong Kong Optometric Association 1 Glenealy, 21st Floor, Flat B. Tel. 5 – 222 893.
INDIA.	The Indian Optometrical Society 14/3a Gariahat Road, Calcutta 700019. Tel. 24 07 97. Indian Optometric Association Post Box 2812, New Dehli 110060. Tel. 567 662.

IRELAND.
Association of Optometrists Ireland
10 Merrion Square,
Dublin 2.
Tel. 616933.

ISRAEL.
The Israel Optometric Association
1A Arlozoroff Street,
Haifa.
Tel. 660073.

ITALY.
Societa Italiana d'Optometria
225 Corso Alfieri,
P.O. Box 193.
1 – 14100 Asti.
Tel. (0141) 53688.

JAPAN.
Japan Optometric Association
2 – 5 – 5 Izumi Higashiku,
Nagoya 461.
Tel. (052) 9332 – 0610.

KOREA, South.
Opticians Association of Korea
12 – 1 Namdaemunno 5 ga,
Chung – gu,
Seoul.
Tel. (02) 778 – 1986.

NEW
ZEALAND
New Zealand Optometrical
Association
P.O. box 31.164,
Lower Hutt 6301.
Tel. 04–698–722.

PORTUGAL.
U.P.O.O.P.
Campo Grande 286 – 2 – Dto,
1700 Lisboa.
Tel. 759 2937.

SINGAPORE.   Singapore Optometric Association
02 – 15 Peace Centre,
1 Sophia Road,
Singapore 0922.
Tel. 377 6821.

SOUTH AFRICA. South African Optometric Association
P.O. Box 3966,
0001 Pretoria.
Tel. (012) 21 7438/9.

SPAIN.   Colegio Nacional de
Opticos-Optometristas
Princesa No. 25 – 1,
Madrid 28008.
Tel. (91) 247 4851.

SWEDEN.   Sveriges Leg. Optikers Riksforbund
Arstaangsvagen I C,
S – 117 43 Stockholm.
Tel. 08 18 07 75.

SWITZERLAND. Schweizerischer Optikerverband
Baslerstrasse 32
Postfach.
Ch 4601 Olten.
Tel. 062–3280–33.

UNITED
KINGDOM.   Association of Optometrists
Bridge House,
233 Blackfriars Road,
London, SE1 8NW.
Tel. (01) 261 9661.

British College of Optometrists
10 Knaresborough Place,
London, SW5 0TG.
Tel. (01) 373 7765/7.

U.S.A. American Optometric Association
243 North Lindbergh Blvd,
St Louis,
Missouri 63141.
Tel. (314) 991 4100.

Chapter 12
Insuring your Lenses

There are two ways of reducing the cost of replacing lenses when they are lost or broken. You can insure with an insurance company or you can join a replacement scheme organised by your practitioner.

When you insure with an insurance company you pay a premium to cover accidental loss or accidental breakage of the lenses. Usually you cannot claim when the lens wears out! The insurance company carries a loss when you claim and you are required to pay a re-instatement premium after a claim.

When you join a replacement scheme you pay the practitioner an annual service fee. This may be just for the replacement scheme or it may include a number of visits when it will be called an annual care plan. An annual care plan incorporates a charge for the practitioner's time and responsibilities involved in replacing lost, broken or worn out lenses.

The differences between a replacement scheme and insurance can be listed as follows:

1. Replacement schemes replace lenses for any reason but especially if the lens is worn out whereas insurance only covers accidental loss and breakage.

2. Replacement scheme fees pay for the practitioner's time and expertise in replacing lenses when required whereas insurance companies premiums cover any claim and pay the practitioner the full replacement cost including his fee.

3. Replacement schemes do not underwrite a loss when the lenses are replaced because the lenses are supplied at a figure above cost price.

4. Insurance companies do not encourage claims whereas the practitioner operating a replacement scheme will encourage you to change your lenses on a regular basis.

5. There is no paperwork involved when ordering a lens through a replacement scheme whereas a claims form has to be submitted to an insurance company with the inevitable delays this brings.

6. Insurance companies increase the premiums if you are a bad risk and may even refuse renewal.

It is because of point 4 that replacement schemes have become very popular. Insurance companies premiums are high because claims are frequent. It is very easy to lose a lens when it starts to wear out!

There are some insurance companies which deal specifically with contact lens insurance and others may allow an extension to normal household policies.

If you can, it is sensible to insure with a company that your practitioner knows so that he can help you when a claim is made. Ask his advice as to whom he recommends and the amount of cover required every time you renew.

Chapter 13
I.D. Cards

There are two useful bits of information that you could carry around with you on a special identity card. This should be filled in by your practitioner.

If you were to have an accident and be knocked unconscious it is very important that rescuers should know whether you are a contact lens wearer and whether the lenses should be removed. If you carry the card at the back of the book, it would be very helpful. As you can see I have combined this card with a normal donor card. You can keep it all or cut it in two.

Once this I.D. card has been filled in ask your practitioner to stamp the back of the card with his practice stamp then fold it up and put it in your wallet or purse.

Glossary of terms used

Aberration

A distortion seen through a lens. Non-convergence of rays of light.

Aftercare

A never ending period of time needed to check eyes and lenses after they are fitted.

Allergy

Abnormal sensitivity reaction of the body to substances that are usually harmless.

Anterior Chamber

Area between the cornea and the iris filled with fluid called aqueous humour. Usually about 3mm deep.

Aphakia

Condition of eye where crystalline lens has been removed.

Astigmatism

Normal condition where the eyeball is not spherical.

Bifocal

Lens that focuses for distance and reading.

Cataract

Name given to crystalline lens when it becomes opaque.

Cones

Colour-sensitive nerve endings in retina.

Conjunctiva

Transparent skin on front of eye covering the white of eye and underside of eyelids.

Conjunctivitis.

Inflammation of conjunctiva.

Convergence

The turning in of the eyes to focus on close objects.

Cornea

Transparent window at front of eye that is responsible for two-thirds of the focusing of the eye.

Corneal Lens

Contact lens that sits within the boundaries of the cornea. Usually a rigid lens.

Corneal Ulcer

An open sore on the cornea that may discharge puss and has to be medically treated.

Cosmetic Lens

Lens used to cover unsightly eye or to change the appearance of the eye.

Crystalline Lens

Variable lens inside the eye behind the iris responsible for one third of the focusing of the eye and changing the focus from distance to reading.

Dispensing Optician

An optician who makes up spectacles or fits contact lenses to a written prescription.

Disposable Lenses

Contact lenses with a limited lifespan of one to two weeks.

Extended Wear

Keeping lenses in overnight on a regular basis.

Extended Wear Lenses

Lenses designed to be kept in overnight.

Eye Muscles

Muscles that move the eyes up and down, left and right, inwards and raise the eyelids.

Fenestration

Hole drilled through contact lens to increase tear flow.

G.P.C.

Giant papilliary conjunctivitis. Toxic or allergic condition under eyelids.

Gas Permeability

Amount of air which can go through a lens.

Glaucoma

Condition where internal pressure of the eye increases causing damage to the retina.

Hypermetropia

(LONG SIGHT) Normal eye condition where eye is too small and eyes have to overfocus to see clearly.

Implant

Plastic lens inserted into the aphakic eye during surgery to replace crystalline lens that has been removed.

Iris

The coloured part of the eye that is in fact a diaphram opening and shutting to let in more or less light into the eye. Also opens under other influences (e.g. fear).

Keratometer

(Ophthalmometer) Instrument used to measure the curves on the cornea.

Lacrimal Gland

Gland above the eye in the orbit that supplies tears.

Liquid Lens

Lens made of tears trapped between the contact lens and the cornea.

Macula

Curved spot at the centre of the retina where 'cones' are concentrated to give very accurate sight and colour vision.

Meibomian Glands

The major glands on the eyelid margins that supply mucous into the tears.

Micro-Corneal

Name given to rigid lenses less than 8mm in diameter.

Myopia

(SHORT SIGHT) Normal eye condition where the eye is too

	big and cannot focus into the distance.
Myopic Creep	Increase in myopia induced by contact lenses.
Nystagmus	A condition of the eye where the eye wobbles uncontrollably and vision is poor as a result.
Ophthalmic Optician	Name given to opticians who examine eyes. Now almost obsolete as the name OPTOMETRIST is used.
Ophthalmic Medical Practitioner (U.K.)	Doctor who examines eyes.
Ophthalmologist	A doctor who specialises in treating eye disease.
Ophthalmic Surgeon (U.K.)	An ophthalmologist who also carries out eye surgery.
Ophthalmoscope	An instrument used to examine the inside of the eye through the pupil.
Optic Nerve	Second cranial nerve that carries information from the retina to the brain.
Optometrist	An optician who specialises in examining eyes and prescribing optical appliances such as spectacles and contact lenses.

Periodic Cleaner   A cleaner used less frequently than a daily cleaner.

Perspex   Trade name (ICI) for acrylic resin.

Presbyopia   (OLD SIGHT) A normal condition of the eye that occurs when the crystalline lens ages. The eye loses its ability to focus from distance to reading gradually over a twenty year period.

Prism Ballast   Specifically making a lens with a thin top and a thick bottom so that it is heavier at the bottom.

Polaroid   Trade name for polarizing type of sunglass lens that cuts out the glare from the surface of water. Ideal for sailors and fishermen.

Posterior Chamber   Small area between the crystalline lens and the back of iris.

Pupil   The aperture into the eye that appears black because it is a hole. Gets smaller with bright light and bigger in the dark.

Reduced Optic   The process by which a lens is made thinner by making the centre smaller.

Registered Optician Term used in the U.K. to describe a practice where both optometrists and dispensing opticians work together.

Retina The layer at the back of the eye that has millions of light-sensitive nerve cells connecting to the brain via the optic nerve.

Retinal Blood Vessels The transparent blood vessels that supply the retina which are seen with the ophthalmoscope during an eye examination.

Retinoscope An instrument used to reflect light off the retina so that the prescription can be gauged objectively.

Rigid Lens A hard lens rather than a soft lens.

Rods Light sensitive nerve cells in the retina that tell light from dark. Responsible for night vision.

Sclera The white, tough outer coat of the eye.

Slit Lamp The microscope used to examine the front of the eye.

Spectacle Blur Reduced vision noticed particularly with spectacles when contact lenses are removed.

Subjective Tests   Tests carried out to fine tune your
                           vision and muscle co-ordination
                           where you have to say what you
                           see.

Suction Holder   A rubber sucker used to remove
                           contact lenses.

Surfactant   Cleaner used to scrub surface of
                           contact lens.

Tonometer   Instrument used to measure
                           internal eye pressure.

Toric Lens   Contact lens specially shaped to
                           correct astigmatism.

Toxic Reaction   Red eye caused by chemicals.

Truncation   Special edge shaping to stop lens
                           rotating on the eye.

Ultra-Violet   Harmful end of spectrum light,
                           which causes ageing of the eye.

Vitreous Humour   Transparent jelly filling globe
                           between chrystalline lens and the
                           retina.

Water Content   Amount of water in a soft lens
                           presented as a percentage.

Donor Card

Keep the card with you at all times in a place where it will be found quickly

- -

Name

Address

Telephone Numbers

I wear................ contact lenses. In emergency, the lens should be removed/left in. My practitioner may be contacted on............

If there is no alternative, please put my lenses in a sealed container with fresh, cold tap water.

I request that after my death

*(a) my *kidneys, *eyes, *heart, *liver, *pancreas be used for transplantation, or

*(b) any part of my body be used for the treatment of others

*(delete if not applicable)

Signature   Date

Full Name (block capitals)

In the event of my death, if possible please contact

Name   Telephone

PRACTITIONER STAMP